BATTLEFIELD ESSEX

A relic from the Second World War. Two of the remaining towers of Shivering Sands fort located midway between Essex and Kent in the Thames Estuary. Originally built as anti-aircraft gun platforms but later fought over by radio pirates

Police battle striking miners.
Wivenhoe Port, May 1984
Image courtesy of the East Anglian Daily Times

BATTLEFIELD
ESSEX

Andrew Summers
John Debenham

Essex Hundred Publications
Rutland House
90 – 92 Baxter Avenue
Southend-on-Sea
Essex SS2 6HZ
www.essex100.com

BATTLEFIELD ESSEX
First published June 2017
Written by Andrew Summers and John Debenham
© Copyright Andrew Summers and John Debenham
June 2017

ISBN 9780993108341

Typeset by Hutchinson Creative
Printed by 4edge Publishing
22 Eldon Way
Eldon Way Industrial Estate
Hockley Essex SS5 4AD

Contents

List of Illustrations

All other maps and images are from the Essex Hundred Collection

Period newspaper clippings courtesy of British Newspaper online archive and Essex Libraries.

Every effort has been made to contact copyright holders of images reproduced in this book. If any have been inadvertently overlooked the publisher will be pleased to make restitution at the earliest opportunity

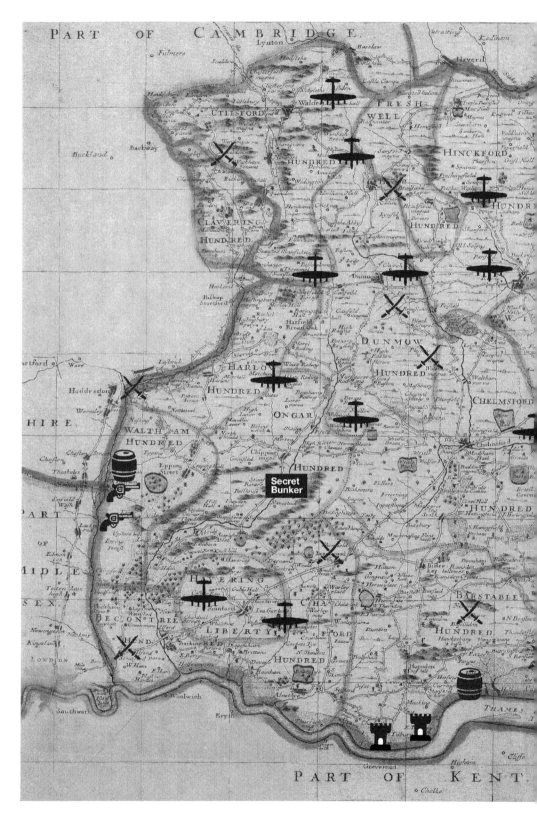

KEY

✕ Battle

✈ Wartime Airfield

⚓ Seafort

🏰 Defensive Fort

🔫 Arms Manufacture and explosive

🛢 Explosive Manufacture

Secret Bunker

Acknowledgements

In bringing this book to publication we have benefited greatly from the help of curators, archivists, editors, librarians and many others throughout the county. Without them the book would not have been possible and we are indebted to them.

Establishing the detail of some of the events we record has been a complex process. Researching material from the past is always a challenge. Many of the original ancient records have disappeared either through neglect, accident or deliberate destruction. As a consequence many events have been reinterpreted by chroniclers often many years after the event happened. The *Anglo-Saxon Chronicles* are a major historical source for the 200 years prior to AD 1,000. However, its description of key events such as the Battle of Benfleet, limited to just a few sentences and almost impossible to cross check, has had to be interpreted in the light of later scholarly research and archaeological evidence.

Sometimes even more recent history proves difficult to interpret and to this end we are particularly grateful for the assistance of Tony Hill, the Military Archivist at Shoeburyness, in helping to clarify the time lines for the weapons testing ranges at that location. We would also like to thank Les Pearce, the Regimental Secretary of the Military Provost Staff Association at Berechurch Hall Camp, for showing us the fascinating items on display from times past at the former WW2 POW Camp 186.

Specials thanks are also due to Glenis Summers for her proof reading and insightful suggestions. Whilst we have taken every care to check facts, and visit the locations mentioned where possible, we are aware that we are fallible. For any errors found in our text we humbly apologise.

Should any reader feel able to provide additional information to enlighten us on any chapters in the book, their comments would be most welcome and we offer our thanks in advance.

INTRODUCTION

Battlefield Essex is the eighth book we have produced in the Essex Hundred series and we are pleased to say that most of the titles are still in print and available from book shops or cyber retailers.

Although part of the title is *Battlefield,* this is not a military reference book. In the last 2,000 years there have been a number of bloody battles on Essex soil but there have also been several conflicts that, although sometimes violent, didn't involve the loss of life. In many cases these conflicts have been hyped in contemporary media as 'battles' and the term has stuck. The prime example of this was the long running dispute in Thaxted in the 1920s in what was known as the 'Battle of the Flags'. To our knowledge, although there was damage to property, no one was killed or even seriously injured during this battle.

Apart from the battles, Essex has been a front line county in England since the time of the Saxons and the Viking raiders 1,500 years ago, so accordingly it is proper to examine the various defences put in place to thwart potential invaders and to look at whether these forts and other defensive measures were much of a deterrent. Fortunately, in recent times, what might be called 'foreign' invaders have never set foot in Essex. Nevertheless the county, with its munitions factories and arms development and weapons testing facilities, has played a major part in the defence of the realm during the course of both World Wars, as well as suffering from the effects of enemy bombings.

As the tide of World War II swung in favour of the allies, Essex became a launching pad to strike the enemy. The US Air Force arrived in strength and stately homes were requisitioned by the military to train forces for clandestine missions in occupied Europe. Following the end of World War II (a hot war), a cold war commenced almost immediately and a site near Ongar became a key installation for planning the aftermath of a nuclear strike.

As with all our Essex titles we include the part of Essex that is now in London, what we call 'Metropolitan Essex'. The county was founded as the Eastern Kingdom of the Saxons and its name derives from the Old English 'Eastseaxe'. This kingdom may also have included parts of modern Hertfordshire and Middlesex.

The county's natural borders; the River Stour to the north, the North Sea to the east, the Thames to the south and the River Lea to the west, were well established when England became a united kingdom under the rule of King Alfred over 1,000 years ago. They remained more or less intact until the creation of the Greater London Council in 1965. This resulted in long established councils such as Romford, Hornchurch, Chingford, Ilford, Walthamstow, Leyton and Woodford disappearing into the new larger authorities of Havering, Redbridge, Barking and Dagenham and Waltham Forest as the case may be. Even West Ham and East Ham, which had functioned with looser Essex ties for several years, became part of the London Borough of Newham. At the same time North Woolwich, which was part of Kent, although north of the River Thames and geographically in Essex, was also transferred to the London Borough of Newham.

The reorganization brought relatively little change to the land area of Essex. The five new boroughs accounted for less than eight percent of the original 'Saxon' Essex. However, in terms of population it was a different matter. At a stroke over one million people, or 40% of the Essex population, became Londoners.

In writing this book it was never our intention to create an academic reference work. In *Battlefield Essex*, as in our other Essex Hundred titles, we have done our best to record not only some of the memorable events, people and places but also the part they played in various conflicts, real and potential, that have shaped the county of Essex.

Andrew Summers
John Debenham

THE RIDDLE OF BOUDICCA

A triumphant Boudicca. The statue was erected nearly 2000 years after her victory

Boadicea, her Latin name, or Boudicca, her Celtic name, is one of Britain's greatest heroines. Much of the romantic myth surrounding her was created by the Victorians. It is exemplified by Thomas Thornycroft's statue of a triumphant Boadicea and daughters in her chariot. Standing on the Thames Embankment by Westminster Bridge, opposite the Houses of Parliament, this statue celebrates Boudicca's defiant rebellion against Roman occupying forces nearly 2,000 years ago. Thomas Thornycroft, died in 1885 and the statue was erected 17 years later.

Although Boudicca's Iceni tribe were based in Norfolk, her rebellion really got under way with an attack on the Roman regional centre of Camulodunum – modern day Colchester in Essex.

When Prasutagus, King of the Iceni, died in 59 AD, he left half of his kingdom and wealth to his Queen and two daughters; the other half to the Roman rulers. This arrangement had been acceptable to previous Roman governors and was meant to assure that peace prevailed. This time, however, area commanders rejected the plan and demanded everything become theirs. Boudicca's refusal to comply ended with her being publicly flogged and her two daughters raped. The simmering rage among the Iceni came to a head in AD 60 and Boudicca led an avenging army to attack Roman Colchester. The colony was a major centre of Roman authority and considered a favourite place for retired soldiers to live. With minimal defences, since attack was not considered likely, the town was overrun by the superior numbers of the Iceni, razed to the ground and all the inhabitants massacred.

Boudicca's forces, now swollen by the Trinovantes of Suffolk and Essex, then swept south-westward following the Roman road, more or less today's A12, to attack the smaller, but vitally important commercially, colony of London (Londinium). With the local garrison away fighting in Wales, London was poorly defended and met the same fate as Colchester. The rebel army by now, according to the Roman historian Tacitus, numbered over two hundred thousand. Emboldened by their victories they headed for the strategically important Roman base of St. Albans (Verulamium). Like London, St Albans was poorly defended and suffered the same fate.

Archaeological evidence is conclusive that Colchester, London and St Albans were destroyed and burned to the ground about 2,000 years ago. Evidence of the burning survives in what is known as 'Boudicca's Destruction Horizon'. Excavations in all three locations have revealed a thick layer of red soot, as well as artefacts showing evidence of severe scorching. There is a glass panel in the cellar of the George Hotel in the High Street, Colchester, through which this distinctive burnt red clay can be seen.

The destruction of these three important towns suggests that the Romans had severely underestimated the strength of the Iceni revolt and the support Boudicca's army had gathered after the rout of Colchester. The situation was about to change.

After destroying Verulamium, Boudicca's army, now allegedly grown to 230,000, moved northwards, intent on further ridding the country of Roman rule. Over confident from easy victories, undisciplined and ill equipped compared to the Romans, they fell into a carefully laid trap set by the, now highly organised, Roman Commander Suetonius Paulinus. The Britons were annihilated and the revolt was over. Boudicca is said to have died by taking poison to avoid capture.

The site of this final battle has led to much speculation. Staffordshire, Cambridge, Worcester and the East and West Midlands have been suggested, along with Surrey and even London's Kings Cross. One popular twentieth century myth suggested that Boudicca is buried under platform 8 or 9 at Kings Cross Station!

Much of what we know of Boudicca is legend. We do not know when she was born, who her parents were or even exactly where she came from. In fact, apart from being the widow of King Prasutagus of the Iceni tribe of East Anglia, we know very little. Even the name of our heroine is shrouded in mystery. The only known source of her British tribal name of 'Boudicca' comes from the Roman historian Tacitus. Other versions such as 'Boadicea' or 'Buduica' have come from mistranslations over the years from the Greek 'Θρίαμβος'.

All our knowledge of Queen Boudicca's revolt has come from only two second hand accounts written by Romans at least 40 years after the event. There are no known 'British' records of the insurrection.

The first of these sources is the Roman historian Publius (or Gaius) Tacitus who was perhaps four or five years old when the revolt broke out. Some 40 years later his book *Agricola* was published, followed by *the*

Annals of Ancient Rome. Agricola is a semi-biographical account of Julius Agricola, a Roman Officer who served under Suetonius throughout the revolution. The second source, published nearly 150 years later by the Greek Roman Historian, Dio Cassius, and written in Greek, is *Romaika*, a history of Rome.

Thus all the 'facts' on Queen Boudicca have come from the 'other' side and were written in Latin or Greek. Over the centuries these works have been translated, reinterpreted and retranslated several times, regularly copied, frequently inaccurately and with large parts missing. Most of the original manuscripts have disappeared. Certainly it was a case of the 'victors writing the history' after the event. Roman historians had to be careful when recording events. If their version conflicted with the views of their masters, the consequences could be serious. Possibly at great risk, Tacitus documented the injustices suffered by Boudicca at the hands of the Romans in some detail. However, he balanced this in his graphic accounts of atrocities committed by Boudicca's forces when they sacked Colchester and London.

Although Boudicca's attack on Colchester and London are well documented many questions remain. The size of Boudicca's army is suspect; how and when did it travel from Colchester to London? Tacitus wrote of her army initially numbering 100,000 and doubling in size by the time it reached London. Travelling overland from Colchester, even following the Roman road, would have been a huge logistical exercise for such numbers.

Essex at that time was mostly forested and had no other roads to speak of between London and Colchester. Every single river and stream, and there were many, would have presented a major obstacle. As the army approached London the problems would have multiplied. The area that is Romford and Ilford today was then densely forested. Rivers like the Roding and the Lea would have been exceedingly difficult to cross, not only for people but also for fighting chariots, baggage wagons and pack animals. These rivers were not then the tightly embanked waterways of today. They grew and shrank over wide flood plains, with the tides or seasons, creating marshes either side covering much of present day Stratford, Walthamstow and Barking all the way to the banks of the River Thames.

Did the march on London take place in the short, wet and cold days of winter, in early spring or in the long warm days of summer? What was the state of the Roman road? How long did it take for an army of one to two hundred thousand? It's conceivable that the vanguard could have arrived close to London whilst the rearguard was still departing from Colchester. According to Tacitus, Boudicca's decision to attack London was made in the heat of the moment after the destruction of Colchester so it would seem that no advance planning was made for the overland journey of some 60 miles.

Can Tacitus' account of the size of Boudicca's Army be trusted? He cites rebel army figures of between 100,000 and 230,000 with 80,000 being killed during the final battle. There are no reliable estimates for the size of the English population before 1813 when the first census was undertaken. Analysis of the *Domesday Book* (compiled around 1068) suggests a population of less than two million. As Boudicca's revolt took place 1,000 years earlier it is quite likely the 'British' population would have been far smaller. Based on this it would seem virtually the whole population of England would have been in Boudicca's Army. Since the rebel forces were drawn mainly from the East Anglian, Iceni and Trinovantes tribes, the Roman accounts of the numbers in the rebel army seem at best grossly exaggerated, at worst quite implausible.

As to the final battle, to date, no mass graves supposedly containing the remains of tens of thousands of bodies and their weapons, that might confirm its location, have been unearthed. Where Boudicca's forces made their final stand remains a mystery. In the light of these many unanswered questions about this revolution, the story of Boudicca or Boadicea, as a celebrated Celtic queen, wife, and mother is destined to remain a historical mystery.

THE VIKINGS ARE COMING

Following the collapse of the Roman Empire, the Anglo-Saxons arrived in the British Isles around 450AD. The Anglo-Saxons came mainly from lands that are in present day Germany, Denmark and Holland. The Angles settled in East Anglia and the Saxons in areas of Sussex (South Saxons), Middlesex (Middle Saxons), and Wessex (West Saxons). They also settled in Essex, a name considered to be derived from the East Saxons.

For the next 400 years there were no recorded battles in Essex but by the ninth century England was the object of sporadic invasion and subsequent settlement by Vikings and later Essex became the scene of a series of decisive encounters. In 892 Danish forces mounted a major attack on Wessex, the part of England ruled by Alfred the Great. Their intention was to take control of the whole country. The main Danish fleet of 250 ships landed their 'Great Army' on the south coast of Kent and set up base near Ashford. At the same time the Viking chieftain, Haesten 'The Black', with a smaller fleet of 80 ships, arrived on the Isle of Sheppey in the Thames estuary. However, Alfred's forces, forewarned of the invasion, struck first and forced Haesten to flee across the Thames to the Danish settlement of Beamfleote (now South Benfleet). This success enabled Alfred to move on to engage Viking forces further south in Kent.

A Danish community of shipwrights had been established at Beamfleote for some years. Its name meant wood and water. Surrounded by forest, with fresh water from two streams, it was hidden from the estuary's main stream. Tidal marshes prevented surprise seaborne attack. Haesten found it a perfect base from which to launch raids around the coast, into Kent and even up to London. After strengthening the settlement's defences and mounting a garrison guard, Haesten set off on raiding activities further afield.

Meanwhile elements of 'The Great Army', which was losing ground to King Alfred in the Weald of Kent, fearing capture, fled and made their way to the relative safety of Benfleet where they considerably bolstered the garrison. The possibility of this becoming a strong Viking military base set alarm bells ringing in Saxon quarters. King Alfred's son Edward and son-in-law Ethelflaed raised a fresh army in London and marched east along the Thames, keeping to forest tracks. Marshalling their forces on the high ground of Hadleigh, they swooped on the unsuspecting Danes at Benfleet, storming the fort. Despite the reinforcements Haesten's men were routed. Many survivors fled overland to the Danelaw settlement at Shoebury, but Haesten's wife and two children were captured and taken to London. With the fort vanquished, many of the Viking ships were burned. Later Alfred ordered Haesten's family to be returned to him in exchange for his promise never again to attack England.

Archaeological surveys have pinpointed the probable site of the Viking ships' anchorage. It runs from the Canvey side of the railway bridge, through to the drainage streams of 'Church Creek', behind St Mary's Church and comes up behind the *Anchor* Pub to the back of 'The Moorings' Hall. It is the area from the railway bridge to the *Helmet and Hoy* that is a likely site for the burning of the ships. As to Haesten's Fort, it is thought likely to have been built within the confines of the car park near Benfleet station, between School Lane and the High Street.

The so called **Battle of Benfleet** is commemorated by a stone sculpture by Anthony Lysycia which stands in the conservation area between Ferry Road and Benfleet Creek.

In terms of numbers engaged it was not a major battle, but it was decisive in marking the beginning of the end for the Danish dominence in Essex for 100 years. Yet the Vikings were not done. Three years later, in 895, a major Viking invasion targeted London. The *Anglo-Saxon Chronicles* records that a substantial force of Danish (Viking) raiders decamped from Mersea Island off the Essex coast in the Blackwater Estuary. They took to their long ships and sailed south to the Thames estuary. Their objective was to overrun and destroy London and with it the authority of Alfred, the Anglo-Saxon King. The Danish fleet of at least 100 vessels carried some 3,000 warriors. Whilst the number of fighters was relatively small, equivalent to four or five modern day battalions, in Anglo-Saxon England it posed a real threat. The Danish fleet left Mersea early in the year, an odd choice considering the short days and inclement weather. After pausing at Shoebury to regroup and obtain supplies and fresh water, the fleet turned west into the River Thames and headed towards London.

They passed the ruins of the camp at Benfleet but progress up the Thames was difficult and slow. The Viking long ships were weighed down with fighting men, weapons and armour. They also carried huge amounts of supplies, animals and plunder from previous raids as well as women and children. Although most of the ships were under sail, a great deal of physical effort was still needed to make headway, especially against the outgoing tide. Many of the vessels in the fleet were barely seaworthy following attacks on England's east coast and even forays into France.

The Vikings' movements upstream were monitored by Alfred's spies and the king, based in London, put plans in place to counter the incursion. Realising that he didn't have enough men to fight the Danes head on, he cautiously moved his forces down river, while allowing for a speedy retreat if necessary.

As the vanguard of the Danish fleet reached Bow Creek, opposite the present day O2 Arena, for some inexplicable reason they turned north into the River Lea and proceeded to head up stream. The rest of the Danish fleet obediently followed.

The landscape of the River Lea was very different 1,000 years ago. Whilst most of the land bordering the lower Lea and Thames was unattractive marsh, the middle and upper reaches of the Lea were lush and surrounded by forest.

The Danes pressed on regardless and followed the course of the River Lea through the middle of the area that is today's Olympic Park at Stratford, on past Stoke Newington, Tottenham, Walthamstow, Enfield and Waltham Abbey. They stopped at Ware, in Hertfordshire, 20 miles distant from the River Thames. Although the Lea rises at Leagrave Marsh in Luton, Bedfordshire, 52 miles from where it joins the Thames at Bow, it was impossible for the Danish longships to navigate any further.

Ware itself was a border town between Anglo-Saxon Wessex and the Viking controlled Danelaw. Danelaw was simply a historical name given to the part of England in which the laws of the Danes (or Vikings) held sway. The River Lea was part of the frontier established some years earlier in '*The Treaty of Alfred and Guthrum*' between King Alfred and the Danish King Guthrum which agreed the boundaries of the Danelaw. This may have explained why the Danish captain chose that route. The Danes remained at their base in Ware for six months.

Sensing an opportunity, Alfred's army followed the Danes up the River Lea and attacked the Vikings in their newly fortified compound. It was a disaster. Defeated, and with four of his leading commanders killed,

Alfred retreated to Waltham Abbey. He deployed his remaining forces to protect the gathering of the summer harvest which, should it have fallen into the hands of the Danes, would have had dire consequences for

A replica Viking longship

Londoners. Then he set to work diverting the course of the River Lea. He also built a series of fortifications on either side of the bank at strategic points. The Danes were trapped. They had sailed into a bottleneck and then Alfred had sealed it with a cork.

An 18th century historian, William Robinson, speculated that the 'works' by Alfred to block the Danes' escape were built across the River Lea in Tottenham on the site of today's Tottenham Lock.

The outcome of these actions resulted in a stalemate. The Danish forces were not strong enough to attack London overland. Alfred, in a similar plight, did not have the resources to penetrate their stronghold. It developed into a waiting game. With the onset of winter, the Danish fighting men decamped. Unable to use their ships, they abandoned them and marched west across the country to the River Severn. Perhaps they wanted to link up with, and reinforce, a Danish contingent based there to form a stronger force to attack Alfred from the south west.

Soon after the Danish departure the Anglo-Saxon army marched into the Danish camp and seized whatever of value remained. Some of the Danish ships that were still seaworthy were towed back to London, the rest were burnt. As to the women, children and the sick that were left behind in Ware there are no records as to their fate.

There had been almost 30 years of continuous warfare. This was now followed by nearly a hundred years where, as far as Essex was concerned, the Danes and the English lived in relative peace.

King Alfred the Great died in 899 and his realm stretched roughly south and west of a diagonal line running from Essex to the River Mersey. The country north of this line was known as the Danelaw.

The Viking fleet's unexplained turn into the River Lea and King Alfred's later military success appear to have resulted in the eastern county border of Essex being established on the River Lea. This remained for over 1,000 years until it was changed in 1965.

In 991 the Danish re-conquest of England began again in earnest. Under the command of Olaf Tryggvason, they crushed the Anglo-Saxon forces at **The Battle of Maldon** on August 10th 991. The Vikings had previously attacked Ipswich with a fleet of 90 plus ships. In response the Anglo-Saxon, Ealdorman Byrhtnoth, and his thegns (military commanders) raised an army of between 3,000 and 4,000 to march against the Vikings as they approached Maldon in the River Blackwater estuary.

The Saxons, with Byrhtnoth in command, mustered on the banks of the Blackwater at high tide. They faced, across open water, on Northey Island, a Danish force of at least 2,000 men, led by Olaf. The Danes demanded payment to leave which Bryhtnoth rejected and instead he challenged them to battle. As the tide dropped the causeway connected to the island appeared. The Vikings approached but the narrow causeway was easy to defend. At this point Tryggvason pleaded to be allowed to cross and fight on equal terms. Bryhtnoth agreed. It has been said he did this because he was big hearted and wanted to avoid other settlements along the coast from having to deal with the Vikings.

Whatever Byrhtnoth's reasons the two sides met and outmanoeuvred by the Vikings, Byrhtnoth was killed, as were most of his thegns and many of the English nobility. The Danes also suffered heavy losses such that they had barely enough men to man their boats. Though they were victorious they did not attack Maldon. However, after the battle, King Aethelred 'The Unready', agreed to buy off the Vikings with an estimated payment of more than 3,000kg of silver.

Maldon was a significant battle, with important political results, but it was just one of many fought by regional forces against the Viking armies which marauded across the country in the decades of Aethelred's reign. Maldon is special because it is so well documented in the contemporary poem, *The Battle of Maldon,* and because its battlefield is believed to have been located with an accuracy unusual for the Anglo-Saxon period.

A statue of Byrhtnoth, created by a local sculptor John Doubleday, was erected in October 2006, at the end of the Maldon Promenade. The nine feet high bronze statue looks down the estuary towards the battle site. Around its base are depicted scenes of the battle that was the beginning of the end of Saxon rule.

Twenty-five years later, in 1016, another legendary Viking, Canute or Cnut, routed the English at the **Battle of Ashingdon. The Battle of Assandun (or Essendune)** was fought between Danish and English armies on 18th October 1016. There is disagreement as to whether Assandun may have been Ashdon near Saffron Walden in north Essex or, as long supposed, Ashingdon near Rochford in southeast Essex. There would seem to be a consensus that the latter is the most likely site. That the battle was fought is not in dispute.

The Danish King Cnut, or Canute, after an unsuccessful attack on London, sailed his fleet of 160 ships up the River Orwell. From there Cnut's army created havoc as far south as Kent where they were confronted by King Edmund Ironsides. Forced to retreat into Essex, the Vikings were overtaken by Edmund's army, reinforced by forces under Earl Ealdric of Mercia.

At Ashingdon hill the two armies confronted each other. Not much is known about the events of the battle itself but Edmund would seem, on top of the hill looking down on Cnut, to have had the advantage. His right hand man, Earl Ealdric, was to lead his forces through woods to outflank Cnut, allowing Edmund to charge down trapping Cnut between them.

Unbeknown to Edmund, Ealdric, instead of outflanking Cnut, had betrayed his king and led his forces away from the battle.

The English forces were routed, incurring the death of many of the English nobility. Though the Danes were victorious there were very heavy losses on both sides. As a result of this battle Edmund and Cnut concluded an agreement whereby Edmund would remain King of Wessex and Cnut would be King of the Danelaw until one of them should die. At that point the survivor would become king of the whole of England and his son would be heir to the throne. Six weeks later, on 30th November, Edmund died and Canute became the first king of all England.

As for Ealdric, whose betrayal had cost Edmund the battle, he survived only until December 1016 when he was killed on the new king's orders. It seems Canute was not prepared to trust someone capable of such treachery.

A few years later, in 1020, the completion took place of the memorial church known as St Andrew's Minster, on the hill next to the presumed site of the battle in Ashingdon. The church stands to this day. It is said King Canute attended the dedication of the Minster with his bishops and installed his personal priest, Stigand. The church is now dedicated to Saint Andrew but is believed previously to have been dedicated to Saint Michael, who was considered a military saint. Churches dedicated to him are frequently located on a hill.

In January 2017 a board was erected at the top of the east facing slope outside St Andrew's Minster with a detailed summary of the Battle of Ashingdon complete with a map and illustrations.

Danish rule had undoubtedly supplanted Saxon rule but within 50 years other invaders would arrive that would again change the course of English History.

Opposing armies at Ashingdon

NORMAN SUPREMECY

Beside the present church building,
Inscribed, on a stone lying flat,
'HAROLD KING OF ENGLAND 1066'
Now - 'Not a lot of people know that!'

King Canute (or Cnut and a Danish Viking) was both the English and Danish king until he died in 1035. The succession in Denmark was complicated by internal strife and war with Norway. In England the Saxons who had been given positions of influence by the relatively benign Canute retook the English throne, first under Edward the Confessor, then Harold Goodwinson.

Perhaps the best remembered battle in English history is, 'The Battle of Hastings, 1066'. What has this to do with Essex? On the surface not much, but then the question arises, why was the defeated Harold, described as the last Saxon king of England, who only survived nine months into his reign, come to be buried in Waltham Abbey? The answer to this reveals a curious tale.

The earliest recorded history of Waltham Abbey goes back to King Canute. Towards the end of Canute's reign, in 1034, a large black stone crucifix, or Holy Rood, was discovered by a peasant, after a vision, in the village of Montacute in Somerset. The Danish Lord of Montacute, 'Tovi the Proud', a close advisor to King Canute (Cnut), decreed that the cross be removed to one of the great religious foundations of the country. He ordered it placed on a wagon to be pulled by twelve red oxen and twelve white cows. There was much discussion as to where to go. Canterbury and Winchester were suggested but the beasts refused to move until Tovi remarked that he was going back to Waltham, where he owned a hunting lodge on the banks of the River Lea. Suddenly the cart started to move appearing to push the animals forward. Once moving, the wagon, accompanied by many of the people of Montacute, continued non-stop until it reached Waltham.

Tovi recognising the importance of the cross, built a new church for it, appointed two priests and gave rich endowments for their maintenance. His wife, Gytha, presented precious stones to adorn the cross. Legend grew that just by touching the cross a miracle might happen and Waltham and its cross became a centre of pilgrimage.

On Tovi's death, his son lost some of his estates, including Waltham, which King Edward the Confessor granted to Harold Godwinson, Earl of East Anglia, and the future King Harold. In 1060 Harold, after praying before the cross, was allegedly cured of a paralysis. In gratitude he had a new larger church consecrated.

Harold became king in January 1066, following the death of Edward the Confessor. Although he enjoyed the support of most of the English nobility, King Harold's claim to the crown was contested on two fronts. In September, at Stamford Bridge, he had to fight off a Viking force, led by his brother Tostig Godwinson and Harold Hardrada, King of Norway, who also claimed the crown of England.

No sooner were the Vikings defeated than a more potent threat materialised in Sussex. A Norman army had landed in Sussex to claim the crown for Duke William. Harold hurried south, only stopping at Waltham to prostrate himself before the cross. Whilst he lay there on the ground, legend has it, the figure on the cross is said to have looked away. This was seen as an ill omen but Harold was not told. Because of this the abbey sent two of its most trusted monks, Osegod and Ailric, to accompany Harold to Hastings.

As the Bayeaux Tapestry tells us, in the battle with William's forces Harold was despatched by that famous arrow in the eye. Osegod and Ailric saw the king struck down. When the battle was over they began a painstaking search to find the body. This was very difficult as many of the dead had been stripped and mutilated. Harold's consort 'Edith the Fair' was brought to confirm that the body they found was in fact Harold's.

The two monks then sought the victorious William's permission to take the body to Waltham Abbey for burial. After initially refusing, William eventually relented and Harold's remains were prepared for transportation to Waltham Abbey. On arrival Harold was buried with great honour and to this day a memorial stone marks his grave in the Abbey Gardens.

Waltham Abbey continued to grow, becoming rich from the pilgrims flocking to the Shrine of the Holy Rood. Because of its wealth it was a prime target for Henry VIII's dissolution of the monasteries. In

1540 the abbey was dissolved and many of the buildings demolished. As for the stone cross, it disappeared at this time and has not been seen since.

Harold's death (centre) as depicted on the Bayeux Tapestry

RAMPAGE

The Norman dynasty survived barely 90 years in England. In 1154 Henry II came to the English throne as the first of the Plantagenet kings, beginning a dynasty which would rule England for over three hundred years and provide fourteen of its kings. Like the Normans, the House of Plantagenet had its origins in France, although from Anjou in the west. In the 16th century they were described by the author and statesman Francis Bacon as, 'a race much dipped in their own blood'. They finally destroyed themselves in the bloody struggle we know as the *Wars of the Roses*.

Perhaps none was more steeped in blood than the third Plantagenet king, John, who came to the throne in questionable circumstances in 1199. His 16 year reign was characterised by misrule, failed foreign wars, harsh taxes and rebellion. He is better known for being associated with the *Magna Carta* and a meeting with his barons in 1215 at Runnymede.

The document that became the *Magna Carta* was in essence a charter to curb the king's power which was put to him by rebellious barons. Five of them, and probably John's most forceful opponents, were Essex based - Richard de Montfichet of Mounfitchet Castle, Geoffrey de Mandeville of Pleshey Castle, William de Lanvallei of Colchester Castle, Robert de Vere of Castle Hedingham and their leader Robert Fitzwalter, Lord of Dunmow, who styled himself *Marshall of the Army of God and Holy Church*. John was forced to agree to the charter. Yet within three months of the *Magna Carta* being sealed he reneged on the agreement and declared war on the rebel barons.

Splitting his forces, John travelled north with a band of loyalists to combat northern rebels. At the same time his half-brother, William Longsword, was tasked with quelling rebellion in the south with an army of largely French mercenaries led by a trusted captain, Savari de Mauléon.

With London firmly in rebel hands, and virtually impregnable, de Mauléon and his army turned to Essex and East Anglia. Most of the castles, manors and estates of Essex, with the exception Rayleigh Castle, the seat of Hubert de Burgh, the King's Chief Minister, were in the hands of rebel barons. These mercenaries adopted a particularly savage aspect of medieval warfare, the 'Chevauchée'. This was to spread terror and havoc by burning, pillaging and laying waste to the countryside.

Chevauchée.
Savary de Mauléon at the head of his band of mercenaries

In late December 1215, Mounfitchet Castle, close to Stansted and a short distance from London, was de Mauléon's first target. This was the seat of Richard de Montfitchet who, although only twenty years old, was a fierce critic of the King. The detail of what actually happened when Mountfitchet Castle was attacked is sketchy and conflicting.

A plausible scenario is that, following an ultimatum from Savari de Mauléon, whose mercenaries vastly outnumbered Mountfichet's garrison, the defenders simply surrendered or more likely fled. The castle was ransacked, soldiers taking whatever booty they could, and the surrounding village laid waste. After destroying everything possible and torching any buildings still standing, the army moved on. Fortunately for him Richard de Montfitchet was absent during the attack, probably in London. The next target for the mercenaries lay 15 miles east where Pleshey Castle was also in rebel hands. It was the seat of Geoffrey de Mandeville, one time Earl of Essex. Contemporary chronicles record that on Christmas Eve 1215 Pleshey Castle was attacked. This time however, though the army may have devastated the surroundings, the castle was not destroyed. With de Mandeville absent and the castle garrison vastly outnumbered by the attackers, again no resistance was offered.

The next day, Christmas Day, a band of mercenaries marched from Pleshey twelve miles north to the Cistercian Abbey at Tilty, between Dunmow and Thaxted. The Abbot Ralph of Coggeshall recorded:-

On Christmas Day 1215 King John's soldiers attacked the abbey and broke into the church while Christmas mass was being said. The soldiers ransacked the church, broke into chests and carried off anything of value.

Either as the result of the attack of shortly afterwards several monks were killed. After a few days rest within the relative comfort of Pleshey Castle, de Mauléon moved his forces further east to the Cistercian Abbey at Coggeshall. Again Abbot Ralph of Coggeshall wrote in the *Chronicon Anglicanum*:-

On New Year's Day (1216) at Coggeshall, while the third hour was said, they violently entered the church and led away twenty two horses which were the property of the Bishop of London.

After Coggeshall, de Mauléon's troops marched into Suffolk towards Bury St Edmonds, creating havoc and destruction as they went. Such was the fear they created with their 'scorched earth' policy, most of the people fled the town. Supporters or sympathizers of the barons' cause were pursued towards Ely. If they sought sanctuary in the great cathedral, Ralph of Coggeshall suggested they sought in vain, when he wrote of events at Ely in graphic terms: *They* (the king's men) *made great slaughter, sparing neither age, nor sex, nor the clergy.* Another chronicler described scenes of utter devastation with the king's enemies being imprisoned, tortured, put in chains and made to pay heavy ransoms. Towns, churches and even cemeteries were robbed or desecrated, with livestock being stolen or killed.

The next move for the royal army was to return to Essex and attack Colchester Castle. The castle had been the seat of the Lanvallei family for thirty years when, in 1214, King John commanded its surrender to Stephen Harengood. One of the terms of the Runnymede charter had been the restoration of the castle to William de Lanvallei. The king was at odds with much of the nobility of England and William de Lanvallei was no exception. He was committed to the rebel cause. Once restored in the castle, Lanvallei brought in his own men and further strengthened the castle defences. The garrison was also reinforced by a French contingent loyal to the rebel cause.

Savary de Mauléon and his men arrived in Colchester in late January 1216. Colchester, however, was unlike the lightly defended Montfitchet or Pleshey castles, or the undefended Tilty and Coggeshall Abbeys. It was a substantial stone built castle, heavily fortified, and its well supplied garrison was determined to keep the stronghold. De Mauléon inspected the castle and issued some threats. A few half-hearted sorties were made to test the defences but these were easily brushed off by the soldiers manning the castle walls. Eventually de Mauléon came to the conclusion that attempting to take Colchester Castle with the forces at his disposal was not going to be possible. For a few days he created havoc in the town of Colchester itself before moving off to rendezvous with King John who was travelling south from battling with the northern barons. John and de Mauléon met in Suffolk and decided to attack nearby Framlingham Castle with their combined forces. Framlingham was the seat of Roger Bigod, the 2nd Earl of Norfolk. This was also a strongly fortified castle which would take a lengthy and bloody campaign to capture.

However, Bigod and his family, having heard of the king's approach, departed for London, leaving the castle in the hands of his constable, William Lenveise. King John, unaware of Bigod's departure, sought to win control of the castle by a process of carrot and stick, rather than to destroy all before him. The carrot was that if the earl surrendered, swore allegiance to the king and above all paid a levy, he and his family would be spared. The castle and all his lands would still be forfeit and in all probability the earl and his close family would be sent into exile. On the other hand, failure to surrender would bring the full might of the king to bear with little expectation of mercy.

Lenveise was placed in an unenviable catch 22 situation. He could not surrender the castle unless given permission but Roger Bigod was out of communication. When the king's envoys arrived to negotiate, Lenveise weighed up the odds and agreed to surrender. The king promptly granted tenure of the castle to Savary de Mauléon. After securing an easy victory at Framlingham, the combined royal forces returned, emboldened, to Colchester Castle, arriving on 14th March 1216. The king had sent envoys in advance to talk to the castle defenders but they had come back empty handed. William de Lanvallei was absent yet the castle defenders, made up of English rebels and French troops, loyal to Prince Louis of France who had been invited by the barons to claim the English crown, seemed in no mood to compromise.

After five days outside Colchester the king withdrew to Ipswich. He returned two days later and offered free passage for the defenders if they surrendered. After some discussion the garrison agreed and on the 23rd or 24th March the castle gates were opened. At this point the king, true to form, reneged on part of the deal. Whilst the 115 French soldiers were allowed to travel freely to London, where they were greeted with extreme suspicion and even calls for them to be hanged as traitors, the Englishmen were shackled in chains and imprisoned. The castle had a new constable, and Stephen Harengood was back.

King John's next move was to seize Castle Hedingham, less than a day's ride from Colchester and home of Robert de Vere, the 3rd Earl of Oxford. He had many grievances against King John and, according to the chronicler Roger of Wendover, was one of the principal promoters of the barons' charter.

Despite its sturdy outwards appearance, Castle Hedingham could not have withstood a determined siege. There was no moat and the main keep, standing on high, dry land, could easily be undermined. Royal forces arrived at Castle Hedingham on 25th March and for once the owner was in residence. Robert de Vere came out to parley with the king. By the 28th March, Hedingham Castle was the king's, together with the considerable de Vere estates. Robert de Vere had to swear allegiance to King John to escape with his life and keep the castle intact.

On 29th March 1216, John's forces moved back to Pleshey Castle, then west across to Canfield near Great Dunmow, Bishops Stortford and finally south to Waltham Abbey, arriving there on 31st March 1216. This phase of the barons' war was at an end. Certainly, as far as Essex was concerned, royal authority had been re-established, even though the Essex barons, albeit deprived of their castles, had all continued the fight, remaining in London which was still firmly in the rebels' grip.

The subjugation of Essex had been achieved by the use of terror. As in wars throughout the ages it was the 'ordinary' people, peasants and villagers, that suffered the most. It would take generations for the countryside to recover. However as far as the barons of Essex were concerned they were all conveniently absent when their castles were attacked, except for Robert de Vere who gave up Hedingham to save his life.

King John died in October 1216 and his nine year old son was crowned King Henry III. Although the rebel cause was eventually defeated, all the Essex barons survived, excepting Geoffrey de Mandeville who was killed in a jousting accident. After swearing allegiance to the new king, who had issued a revised version of the charter that became known as the *Magna Carta*, they all had their lands and castles restored to them.

THE GREAT REVOLT

In May 1381 England was recovering from the 'Black Death', a plague that killed between one third and half of the population. Fourteen year old Richard II was the reigning monarch and the 8th Plantagenet king. He had succeeded his grandfather Edward III, one of whose legacies was the so called '100 years' war with France. The war was not going well. It was also expensive and the majority of the army overseas had not been paid for months. The decline in population from the 'Black Death' had substantially reduced tax revenues and put a severe strain on the feudal system that effectively obliged labourers to work for a specific manorial lord in perpetuity. There was now a labour shortage and in many cases men simply left their manors to find work elsewhere for better wages and conditions, even though this was against the law.

Parliament was determined to raise money. Five years earlier it had introduced a poll tax. This head tax had applied to almost everyone over the age of 14. A second poll tax was levied in 1379 and a third in 1380, charging one shilling, or 3 groats (5p), on all people over the age of 16. It was hoped that the richer elements in society would help the poor; piously expressed at the time as 'the strong might aid the weak'. This was the case in some areas but in many places the tax was a heavy burden.

This latest tax managed to antagonise nearly everyone and led to widespread evasion. New official population figures in Essex in 1381, that already took account of the 'Black Death', suddenly showed a further dramatic decrease from the supposed official figure. This downward adjustment was achieved with the connivance of local civic leaders who simply understated the local population on their returns. Parliament became suspicious and sent commissioners to check on the accuracy of the numbers of people liable to pay the tax.

Tablet on the White Lion at Fobbing

On 30th May 1381, John Bampton, an Essex JP and the Estate Steward of Barking Abbey, was sent to Brentwood with Sir John Gilsburgh MP, the Speaker of the House of Commons, to conduct enquiries into the Barstable Hundred. John Bampton was notoriously corrupt. During his career he had acquired several properties in Essex by dubious means. Sir John Gilsburgh owned many properties in Essex including a large estate and Manor House at Wennington, close to Aveley. He was also an unashamed champion of the war with France and had campaigned energetically in Parliament for additional funds to billet the English army in Brittany during the winter.

The commissioners set up court close to the Thomas à Becket Chapel[i] in Brentwood. On being told by the leader of those summoned, Thomas Baker, that not a penny more would be paid, they ordered his arrest. This resulted in a riot and the commissioners, with their entourage, fled for their lives back to London. Three days later, on Whit Sunday 2nd June, a High Court Judge, Sir Robert Belknap, arrived with the task of restoring order and resuming the enquiry. He was given strict orders to seek out and punish the rioters. However, the Essex men were well prepared.

Rough justice at Brentwood

During the intervening three days messengers had galloped all over Essex and what is now East London, calling for resistance at Brentwood. The mob had now grown to thousands and the Judge's 'hard man' approach only inflamed them further. Riot again ensued. Belknap was manhandled then stripped and made to swear an oath on the bible. He was lucky to escape with his life. Three of his clerks were not so fortunate. They were seized and beheaded, as were some local jurors who were accused of collaborating. Their heads were put on poles for all to see. All the court records were then burnt in a huge bonfire. The incident was a catalyst that sparked the 'Peasants Revolt' or 'Great Revolt' in Essex.

Almost immediately attacks took place all over the county, especially on those associated with authority. As always, criminals and other malcontents used the opportunity to loot and burn and settle scores. The Essex rebels joined with those of Kent, who were led by Wat Tyler[ii], and laid siege to London. The government of Richard II was nearly toppled after the rebels captured the Tower of London, destroyed the Savoy palace, home of John of Gaunt, and in the process killed the Chancellor, the Chief Justice and the Treasurer.

On 15th June two weeks after it all began, Richard II confronted the rebels at Smithfield. Their leader Wat Tyler, who was allegedly worse the wear for drink, died after skirmishing with William Walworth, the Mayor of London, whilst attempting to speak with the king. The young king Richard faced the crowd and won them over with claims on their loyalty and promises of fair treatment.

Following the death of Wat Tyler and the seemingly peaceful dispersal of his followers, the immediate threat to the capital and government was removed. The rebels' joy however was to be short lived. King Richard II moved swiftly to impose his authority. Following the death of the Chief Justice, Sir John Cavendish, killed by the rebels during their assault on the Tower, the king appointed Sir Robert Tresilian in his place. He set up court in Chelmsford with the sole purpose of bringing the instigators of the revolt to justice.

Essex rebels, incensed at being tricked, were not prepared to give up what they believed were their promised new won freedoms. Over two days messages were carried throughout the county demanding that all able bodied men join a general mobilization at Great Baddow and at

Rettendon. Any men not complying were threatened with dire retribution. The response was that hundreds of men assembled with horses and whatever tools or weapons they could muster. They all came together on June 27th; to make a stand in what became known as the **Battle of Norsey Wood.**

The rebels made camp in a field next to Norsey Wood, thought to be in the area of the present Norsey Farm Estate, north east of Billericay. They could not be described as an organised army. They did however dig defensive ditches and construct makeshift barriers of farm carts chained together. Few of them had anything approaching real fighting weapons. Most, at best, had bows and knives, or daggers. The rest made do with traditional tools such as scythes, sickles, pitchforks and staves.

Disastrously, they failed to mount a guard and were taken by surprise before dawn on Sunday 28th June by a well-armed and disciplined force, led by Thomas of Woodstock (Duke of Gloucester, the Earl of Essex and the king's uncle) and Sir Thomas Percy. The king's army charged the rebel camp breaking through the unguarded defences and barricades. They began what can only have been systematic slaughter of the Essex men. The rebels' primitive weapons could not compete with the spears and swords of professional soldiers. With barely time to form ranks those that stood and fought were cut down.

Undisciplined, they broke their barely-formed ranks and the battle became little more than a rout. Many fled into the wood and were hunted down. Some grouped themselves into the old Saxon fighting-rings and made an orderly retreat as best they could but 500 of their number were killed by the king's soldiers. The survivors fled the scene, hopefully to fight another day. Many of the dead were buried in the churchyard at Great Burstead.

The remaining rebels next headed for Colchester to seek support but they had little success. They journeyed into Suffolk only to find the rebellion there already crushed by royal forces. This much diminished band moved on but wherever they turned the king's forces were ready and waiting to pounce. They made their last stand at Ramsey Abbey in Cambridgeshire and suffered heavy losses. The stragglers fled to live their lives as outlaws. As the countryside was secured, the royal court moved from London, first to the Royal Palace at Havering and then to Chelmsford.

From 1st July until 6th July 1381 the king lodged in the Royal Palace[iii] at Writtle and for seven days Writtle became the seat of Government. A swathe of edicts and proclamations were produced and messengers carried them to all corners of the kingdom. Their substance was that the rebellion was over; the only lawful authority was the king or his appointees and all promises made to the rebels earlier were withdrawn as they had been made 'under duress'.

The king's view of the rebels was now, "*Villeins ye are still and villeins ye shall remain*"[iv]. The few elements of the rebellion still active in pockets throughout the country were gradually hunted down by the king's forces.

At Chelmsford, Chief Justice Tresilian promised to spare the lives of those brought before him if the ringleaders were named. Over 145 rebel leaders were identified. Those caught were shown no mercy. After a short trial they were executed and their property confiscated. Included in these was Thomas Baker from Fobbing. Although the status quo more or less returned, things were never quite the same again. There was no doubt the rebellion had rocked the establishment to its core. The Chancellor, the Chief Justice and the Treasurer had all been killed. Several royal lodges and 'Official' buildings had been looted then burned and most of the local records had been destroyed along with them.

In a final twist, perhaps to prevent a recurrence, on 14th December 1381, Parliament declared a general amnesty to all rebels still at large.

(Endnotes)

i   *The remains of Thomas à Becket Chapel are in Brentwood High Street. It was a popular stopping point for pilgrims travelling south on their way to Canterbury in the middle ages.*

ii   *Wat Tyler is remembered today as a hero of the people and is commemorated in Pitsea by the 'Wat Tyler Country Park'.*

iii   *Formerly King John's Palace and now the site of Writtle College.*

iv   *The word Villien is derived from the French or Latin villanus, meaning serf or peasant, someone who is tied to the land and manor of his feudal lord.*

CASTLES

With few exceptions, until 1215 castles in Essex had been built to keep the enemy within the county out, or to protect the ruling classes from disgruntled locals. Castles also served as prisons and a secure base for the baronial lords to sally out and suppress dissidents.

Although traces of earlier defence fortifications have been found in the county it was not until the Norman Conquest that castle building as we know it began. Mostly they were motte and bailey castles. The motte was a mound surmounted by a keep or tower. It was surrounded by the bailey or courtyard which might be up to three acres in size and would house all the resources and people required to run the castle. The bailey would then be surrounded by a wooden palisade and a deep ditch. They were built by Norman barons who had supported William the Conqueror and been rewarded with manors and estates of the conquered Saxons. Clavering Castle, southwest of Saffron Walden is the exception. It was built well before 1066 by Robert Fitz Wymarc, a confidante and advisor to Edward the confessor.

In the hundred years after the battle of Hasting, castles were built in Castle Hedingham, Colchester, Great Canfield, Ongar, Pleshey, Rayleigh, Stansted Mountfitchet, Stebbing and Walden. They were built by generals or commanders that had fought with William at Hastings and been rewarded with grants of the manors and estates of the conquered Saxons. Built fairly quickly and often by forced labour, their function was certainly to defend against possible attack not from invading countries but from the conquered population. The Normans were strangers in a strange land and rebellion was a constant threat. The castles were also symbols of status and power. They provided a secure base from which to administer and control the native inhabitants that had become their serfs or tenants. Most of the castles are now are long gone or are just ruins.

However Stansted Mountfitchet, which was completely destroyed during the time of the first barons' war against King John in 1215, was rebuilt in the 20th century as a replica of the Norman original. The castles at Hedingham and Colchester both survive today in much their original state and along with Stansted Mountfitchet serve as major tourist attractions.

Perhaps the most well-known Essex castle is Colchester. It is the largest surviving example of a stone built Norman keep. It was built on the strategic route between East Anglia and London on the orders of William the Conqueror. It was well placed to thwart invasions from the east coast and London against Scandinavian invaders who were still considered a threat by the Normans. The only other period Essex castle which might claim to have being built to defend the realm was Hadleigh Castle, overlooking the Thames estuary. It was completed sometime after 1230.

Fifteen years earlier King John granted the manor of Rayleigh, which included its castle, to Hubert de Burgh. De Burgh chose to build a new castle at Hadleigh. He considered the enemy within, the Saxons or the rebel Magna Carta barons, had been vanquished so set about building a castle at Hadleigh. Rayleigh castle was then stripped and fell into disuse. Hadleigh was perfectly placed to warn of approaching enemy ships in the Thames Estuary, although it was too far from the water for the garrison to mount any sort of counter attack.

The ruins of Hadleigh Castle

Aubrey de Vere built Castle Hedingham before 1086 when he was given the manor of Hedingham. His son, also Aubrey, built the stone keep which would become the de Vere family seat for more than five hundred years. The de Veres were also the Lords of Canfield. At Great Canfield, near the River Roding, they constructed a motte and bailey castle with a timber keep. Nothing survives except the earthworks. The same construction was used by Eustace II, Count of Boulogne, who built Ongar Castle when he was given the manor of Ongar. Again only earthworks survive.

Another Norman commander at Hastings was William de Mandeville. For his loyalty he was awarded the manor of Pleshey, together with many villages. He built a motte & bailey castle which eventually became a stone castle and the family seat of the de Mandevilles. It fell into ruin in the 15th century. All that remains is the motte which at 15 metres is one of the largest in England.

Rayleigh Castle was built by Sweyn, the son of Robert FitzWymarc of Clavering. Though born in England and one of the wealthiest landowners in Essex, he was a staunch supporter of William and as such was allowed to build his masonry and timber motte and bailey castle in his own manor. All that exists today are the earthwork remains known as Rayleigh Mount.

Henry de Ferrers fought at Hastings and was rewarded with the manor of Stebbing, north-west of Braintree. There he built a simple motte castle of which nothing remains but 'The Mount', a moated earthwork which is a scheduled ancient monument.

The last of these castles, Walden Castle, was built in 1141, at the start of the civil war known as 'the anarchy', by the son of William de Mandeville of Pleshey, Geoffrey de Mandeville, who supported Matilda's claim to the throne of King Stephen. Ordered to surrender his castle, Geoffrey launched an unsuccessful attack on the king's forces in Cambridgeshire. He died the following year, without ever reclaiming his castle. In 1157 Stephen's successor, Henry II, ordered Walden Castle to be 'slighted' – totally destroyed. Today only the ruined core of the castle remains as a scheduled monument and grade 1 listed building. The outline of the bailey may be seen in the layout of Saffron Walden's streets.

THE INVASION THAT WASN'T

The Plantagenet dynasty came to an abrupt end when King Richard III was killed on Bosworth Field in 1483. Henry VII became king and ushered in the Tudor era. He was followed by Henry VIII, Edward VI, Mary I and Elizabeth I. Although there had been numerous plots and rebellions to overthrow the reigning English monarchs they had all been supressed relatively easily and for over 100 years the county of Essex remained largely free of conflict. However, since Henry VIII's break with Rome, external threats to the country had become more pronounced. None more so than in 1588 when the Spanish Armada set sail with the express purpose of returning England to papal authority.

Queen Elizabeth I was the reigning monarch whose rule was defined by the Spanish Armada. Her famous speech, given on a windswept field in Tilbury on, 9th August 1588, included the lines:-

I know I have the body but of a weak and feeble woman; but I have the heart and stomach of a king, and of a king of England.

These were perhaps the most inspirational words ever recorded by a monarch of England when the kingdom was under threat.

A day earlier the queen had arrived at Tilbury Fort which had been built on the orders of her father Henry VIII. She travelled by royal barge from Greenwich and with her entourage made her way to Saffron Gardens, just south of Horndon-on-the-Hill, where she spent the night. The following day Elizabeth headed for the great military camp set up adjacent to the present day Gunn Hill Farm.

Befitting the occasion, the queen rode up, marshal's baton in her hand, clad in white armour on a grey charger. The Earls of Essex and Leicester held the bridle-rein. Assembled were more than 20,000 soldiers standing by to repel any land invasion by forces from Armada ships.

The queen spoke with an unmatched passion.

Let tyrants fear – I come amongst you, not for recreation or sport and famously offered *in the midst and heat of the battle, to live or die amongst you all.* Angrily the queen poured scorn on the papal forces that would dare invade England.

To strengthen defences a boom had been constructed across the Thames between Gravesend and Tilbury to prevent enemy vessels making upstream to London. The watch ships *Victory* and *Lyon* patrolled at strategic points further down the estuary to intercept suspicious craft. The church towers at Fobbing and Leigh-on-Sea served as look out points with their beacon turrets ready to be fired if invaders were spotted.

Ironically the great speech made by Queen Elizabeth took place when, unbeknown to her, much of the threat from the Spanish had been neutralised. Originally the Armada set sail from Lisbon in early July 1588, with 130 ships and some 30,000 men.

The English, through a combination of superior intelligence, better ships and good seamanship, together with favourable weather and good luck, forced the Spanish fleet to take shelter near modern day Calais.

Seizing the opportunity, on 27th July the English unleashed a flotilla of fire ships on the Spanish fleet at anchor which resulted in mayhem. With access to the channel blocked the surviving Spanish ships sailed north and by 29th July had abandoned their invasion plans.

As the prospect of attack receded most of the troops at Tilbury were withdrawn in late August. The remnants of the Armada, forced to sail round the British Isles, finally limped home in mid-September, battered by gales, having lost half the fleet and most of its men.

Queen Elizabeth I inspecting the troops at Tilbury

PLOTTERS

Queen Elizabeth I, the last of the Tudor monarchs, died in March 1603. King James VI of Scotland inherited the English throne through an orderly succession. Uniting England and Scotland, he was crowned King James I of England, the first of the Stuart kings.

Despite the peaceful succession there were several plots to unseat the new king in his first years, the most memorable being the so called *Gunpowder Plot* of 1605. *The Gunpowder Plot* was a failed assassination attempt against the new king by a group of English catholics led by Robert Catesby. The plan was to blow up the House of Lords during the State Opening of Parliament on 5th November.

The plot might well have succeeded if it hadn't been for an anonymous letter addressed to William Parker (Lord Monteagle), an Essex landowner, warning him not to attend the opening of Parliament. On receipt of the letter Parker immediately handed it over to the parliamentary authorities. However, no searches were made until the night before the opening, when 36 barrels of gun powder were discovered in the basement, along with one Guy Fawkes, who was immediately arrested.

Ten miles to the east of the Houses of Parliament, in Barking, lies Eastbury Manor. Legend has it that the Gunpowder Plot was hatched there. At the time Eastbury Manor House was rented to Lewis Tresham, the brother of Francis Tresham, one of the conspirators and also cousin of Robert Catesby, the plotters' leader. Further evidence linking the gunpowder conspiracy to Barking is that on 9th November 1605, just days after Guy Fawkes was arrested, a Barking fisherman named Richard Franklin was questioned by magistrates at nearby Valence House in Dagenham. Franklin alleged that his master, Henry Parish, had hired a boat to Guy Fawkes (who was using the alias Johnson). This boat was used by the plotters for making clandestine trips from Barking along the River Thames to France. Franklin also claimed that Guy Fawkes had made arrangements for the boat to be made ready for his escape once the deed had been done.

The story was boosted just over 100 years later by the author Daniel Defoe. He wrote in his 1727 book *A Tour Throughout the Whole Island of Great Britain:-*

'A little beyond the town, on the road to Dagenham, stood a great house, ancient and now almost fallen down, where tradition says the Gunpowder Treason Plot was at first contriv'd, and that all the first consultations about it were held there.'

Plotters. Guy Fawkes in the centre

Although hard evidence of the gunpowder plotting actually taking place in Barking is open to speculation, what is certain is that 13 conspirators including Guy Fawkes, were apprehended and either killed during their arrest or hung, drawn and quartered after trial and conviction. Eastbury Manor House was purchased by the National Trust after World War II and is now open to the public.

THE SIEGE OF COLCHESTER

The English Civil War began on 22nd Aug 1642 when Charles I (son of James I) raised his standard at Nottingham and formally declared war on Parliament. Four years later the royalist forces were decisively routed at the Battle of Naseby and shortly afterwards the king surrendered to the Scots who promptly handed him over to the parliamentarians. Stuart rule was under threat. It looked as if the parliamentarians, under Oliver Crowell, were in control. However there were still significant pockets of royalist supporters around the country with other ideas. Consequently a second civil war broke out between May and August 1648. Whilst there were no pitched battles on the scale of Naseby, it witnessed a series of sieges and skirmishes where royalist forces were defeated which led to Charles I's eventual trial and execution.

So far Essex had been largely spared from the bloody conflict and in May 1648 the people of Colchester were looking forward to better times. It seemed as if a deal would soon be done and peace would reign. However, the county, and particularly the burghers of Colchester, were about to be disillusioned.

On May 21st 1648, in Kent, a royalist army led by Lord Goring, Earl of Norwich, rose in revolt. Defeated at Maidstone by Lord Fairfax's Roundheads, some 500 of the remnants of this army fled northwards to seek loyalist reinforcements in Essex. At Chelmsford, Colonel Henry Farre, with some of the Essex trained bands, had also declared support for the king under the banner of Sir George Lucas. On the 9th of June they were joined by the Earl of Norwich, Lord Capel, Lord Loughborough and the royalist soldiers from Kent as well as Sir George Lisle and a force from Hertfordshire. This royalist army, with Lucas at its head, marched to Colchester, where on 12th June, their numbers now swollen to 5,500 and knowing they were pursued by Fairfax's army, they decided to stand and fight.

The Burghers of Colchester, terrified of occupation, had barred the gates and posted sixty guards. Lucas, who was a hated former resident, led a charge on the gates; the guards fled and the town was occupied. Colchester now had five and a half thousand extra mouths to feed. Once inside the gates, the Earl of Norwich, confident of more royalist support arriving, announced to the townspeople that he would, "take them into His Majesty's protection and fight the enemy in that situation".

The citizens' worst fears were realized. The town that had been a staunch supporter of Parliament during the first part of the Civil War was now host to an army with which it had very little sympathy; what little there was soon vanished as the soldiers seized already scarce provisions.

Fairfax's army arrived close to Colchester on 13th June where they were joined by an Essex force under Sir Thomas Honywood and Colonel John Barkstead's Infantry Brigade from London. With a total force of over 5,000 experienced troops, plus a thousand cavalry, they decided on an immediate all-out assault on the royalists. The Royalists had posted sizeable forces on the approach roads to the town and established fortifications outside the walls such as St John's Abbey, St Mary's church and the former house of Sir Charles Lucas. Fierce fighting ensued until Fairfax, realizing that, having lost between 500 and 1,000 men, he was not going to be able to take the town by storm, called a halt. Siege was to be his weapon of choice.

The first priority for Fairfax was to isolate the town from the outside world. He ordered forts to be built and siege cannon sited strategically around the town along with earthworks and trenches. Reinforcements, in the shape of six companies of horse and dragoons of the Suffolk trained bands, arrived. They were given the task of guarding the bridges across the River Colne to the north and east. Parliamentary ships were ordered to blockade the harbour and the river mouth to prevent any re-supply via that route.

By 2nd of July the parliamentarians' encirclement of Colchester was complete. Opportunities for the royalists to break out for provisions were severely limited. On 5th July, Lucas with 400 Cavalry and Lisle with 600 infantry attacked the force guarding the East Gate. They took the defenders by surprise but then recklessly ventured too far from the town where they were counter-attacked and suffered severe casualties. The surviving royalists fled back into Colchester empty handed having lost their artillery in the foray. On the night of 14th July, Fairfax ordered an attack on the royalist fortifications that lay outside the town walls. St John's Abbey and the house of Sir Charles Lucas were captured despite fierce defence. St Mary's church was completely destroyed by artillery fire, together with the royalists' main artillery battery. Following this success, on 15ᵗʰ July Fairfax sent a message offering surrender terms. They were rejected out of hand as the royalist commanders were still confident that reinforcements would soon arrive to relieve them. There were several attempts to break out as the siege tightened. Most of the breakouts failed. One that nearly succeeded was when a 1,000 strong force of royalist cavalry made it to Boxted where they fought the two day 'Battle of Boxted Heath', before being forced to withdraw. A successful break out came on 22ⁿᵈ July, when a detachment of Sir Bernard Gascoigne's cavalry escaped via the Maldon road and fled to Cambridgeshire.

The Siege House in Colchester. Still pock marked with bullet holes from the conflict

There was no good news for Lord Norwich and Lucas. The hope for relief was diminishing as one by one royalist forces elsewhere in the country were being defeated. With losses and defections, the royalist force was now down to little more than 3,000 while Fairfax's numbers had grown to over 6,000.

If things were bleak for the royalists they were far worse for the citizens of Colchester. Provisions in Colchester had all but run out. The first horses had been killed for food by the 19ᵗʰ July. By August cats, dogs and even rats had become the staple food. Fairfax applied the siege ruthlessly despite the town's previous loyalty to his cause. The townspeople were not allowed to leave for any reason and nothing was allowed in to them. Petitions from outside the town, pleas from the town council, and even from Lord Norwich, were all to no avail. People were reduced to eating soap and candles and when women and children begged for food at the city gates they were turned away by Roundhead soldiers.

On 24th August news reached Fairfax of Cromwell's victory at the Battle of Preston. He ordered kites to be flown over the town displaying this news in order to destroy any lingering royalist hopes. That same day Fairfax offered Lord Norwich non-negotiable terms of surrender. These stipulated that lower ranks and common soldiers would be granted quarter; senior officers though must surrender to mercy with no guarantee as to how they might fare. Lord Norwich had no alternative but to accept. On 28th August the royalist army laid down their arms and the gates were opened.

When the victorious parliamentary regiments entered the town, with Lord-General Fairfax at their head, they were shocked at the sorry state of both the town and the inhabitants. Cruelly, there was no sympathy for the people; instead they were blamed for allowing the king's men into the town in the first place. The town was only preserved from pillage upon payment of £14,000. The common soldiers were disarmed and issued with passes to return to their homes after they had sworn an oath not to take up arms against Parliament again.

For the time being Stuart rule had come to an end. The fate of the royalist leaders, Lords Norwich, Capel and Loughborough, being of the aristocracy, was left to be decided by Parliament. As for the royalist commanders, Sir Charles Lucas, Sir George Lisle and Sir Bernard Gascoigne, they were tried, found guilty of high treason and sentenced to death. Colonel Farre was also to be tried but he had escaped and Gascoigne was reprieved when he was discovered to be an Italian citizen. Lucas and Lisle were summarily executed by firing squad. A monument to the two men was erected nearly 250 later in 1892 and stands in the grounds of the park behind the castle, (see overleaf).

Monument to Charles Lucas and George Lisle in the grounds of Colchester Castle

DEFENDING THE REALM?
TILBURY FORT

In the 1400s temporary defences had been created at Tilbury to protect shipping routes and the important ferry crossing to Gravesend. This changed in 1539 when a permanent fort, the 'West Tilbury Blockhouse' was built as part of Henry VIII's response to the threat of invasion from France. It was designed to cross-fire with blockhouses on the opposite bank in Kent at Higham and Milton. The French threat never materialised but, fifty years later, there was a new tangible enemy, the Spanish.

The Spanish threat created alarm in England when, in the summer of 1588, their 130 ship strong Armada set out to invade England. The Tilbury Blockhouse was reinforced with two concentric earthwork ramparts surrounded by ditches and a heavy timber palisade. Stretching across the river to Gravesend, anchored to lighters, a boom of ships' masts, chains and cables was laid to defend the capital and an army of 20,000 soldiers was deployed at West Tilbury. On the 8th of August Queen Elizabeth arrived at the fort by barge then rode on to bolster her troops and rally the nation with her famous speech. (see page 42). Yet just like the previous threat from the French, the Spanish didn't arrive either. So it will never be known how the defences would have stood up in the event of attack.

In 1651 Tilbury Fort's garrison, which had held the fort for Parliament in the English Civil War (though it was never attacked) was reported as consisting of a governor, a lieutenant, an ensign, four corporals, a drummer, a master gunner, 16 gunner's mates and 44 soldiers.

There is little to suggest that the fort played any useful part in defending the realm in spite of the huge cost of continually rebuilding and maintaining it. However, in June 1667 its usefulness was seriously questioned when it proved totally ineffective in deterring a Dutch fleet, under the command of Admiral Michiel de Ruyter, which brazenly sailed up the Thames (see page 54) and took full control of the waterway.

Three years after the Dutch incursion, a Dutch engineer, Sir Bernard De Gomme, who was knighted by Charles I for his support in the civil war, was commissioned by King Charles II to redesign and rebuild the fort. Like most projects put in hand by the king the plan proceeded very slowly and many important features were still not incorporated twenty five years later.

Tilbury Fort in about 1831

The writer Daniel Defoe recorded in 1724 that an estimated 100 guns, ranging from 24-pounders to 46-pounders made it, 'A battery so terrible as well imports the consequence of the place'.

Despite this it would seem that the most violence experienced at the fort was a dispute at a cricket match in 1776 between teams from Kent and Essex. The match allegedly ended in bloodshed when guns were seized from the guardroom.

The fort also saw service as a prison when Highland prisoners captured after the Battle of Culloden in 1746 were held there. Later the fort was used as a transit depot and for storing gunpowder.

Tilbury Fort is now run by English Heritage as a tourist attraction.

JUNE 1667 INVASION

In just over 20 years, between 1652 and 1674, the English and the Dutch fought three naval wars. In simple terms the origins of the wars were commercial, coupled with the quest for dominance of the sea routes to the Americas, Africa and the East Indies. Although there were multiple disputes between the two countries that stretched to the far reaches of their emerging colonial empires, nearly all the large scale naval action was confined to the North Sea, the River Thames and the English channel.

The first war began in 1652 when the English and Dutch clashed off the Kent coast. It ended somewhat inconclusively nearly two years later. The English gained the upper hand and Admiral Maarten Tromp, the Dutch fleet commander, was killed in action. However the Dutch were far from vanquished. There followed ten years of an uneasy peace during which time Oliver Cromwell, the architect of the war, had died and the monarchy of Charles II had been restored.

In contrast to the austere regime of Oliver Cromwell, Charles' rule was extravagant and mired in corruption. Although an Anglo/Dutch peace treaty was supposedly in effect, both sides continued to raid each other's far flung outposts. Matters came to a head when Charles authorised his brother James (the Duke of York) to seize New Amsterdam, the present day New York. As a result a second war was officially declared in March 1665.

Initially the English had some success but King Charles's lavish life style, the plague and the Great Fire of London had depleted the exchequer leaving the navy seriously underfunded. There was also considerable infighting within the English admiralty which was exacerbated by the scurrilous writing of the diarist Samuel Pepys. In the autumn of 1666 ferocious gales forced both sides to withdraw. Most of the English fleet made its way to Chatham naval base on the River Medway in Kent. The warships lay at anchor unrepaired and unsupplied. The winter was hard and the river froze over at least twice. Many of the crews deserted. Contractors refused to make repairs unless they were paid in advance and dock workers quit as they hadn't received any wages for months. One ship after another was cannibalised so the fleet shrank. Soon the waters around Chatham were littered with useless hulks that once had been fine fighting warships. In May 1667 Charles decided to order the big ships laid up until further notice. He believed the nation could rely on coastal forts and smaller frigates for defence. Also the king's view, shared by those around him, was that the Dutch were in no state to continue the war.

On the other side of the North Sea the Dutch were busily rebuilding their fleet under the studious direction of Johan de Witt. They were most aggrieved at their commercial fleet being continually attacked by English privateers or the ships of the English navy. Accordingly De Witt and his top admirals meticulously prepared a bold plan to strike at the very heart of the English fleet. The Dutch knew the strength of the coastal forts. They had clandestinely surveyed the approaches to the Thames and Medway. English sailors were released from Dutch prisons and offered positions as pilots or sailors. Even the colonel in charge of the newly formed Dutch Marines was English.

On 7th June 1667 a large Dutch fleet, commanded by Admiral Michiel de Ruyter, set sail for England. Arriving unopposed off the Essex coast the fleet promptly divided in three. One element was left to guard the Thames Estuary approaches, with scouts foraying along the channel to warn of the return of any English squadrons still at sea. A second force brazenly sailed up the Thames, past Hadleigh Castle, almost as far as Tilbury, to block the river, seize merchant ships and prevent any English reinforcements coming from London. The fort at Tilbury, (see page 52) whose purpose was to protect London, proved totally ineffective and the Dutch treated it with disdain. That left a smaller force of 21 ships and support vessels to break off and sail up the River Medway to Chatham to strike at what remained of the English fleet.

On 9th June a Dutch raiding party landed on Canvey Island to collect supplies and fresh water. They took some sheep, burnt a few barns and then left. It seems unlikely that there were any lookouts posted at the ruined Hadleigh Castle although it commanded fine views of the Thames approaches. The invasion had taken England by surprise. The following day, the Dutch easily overran Sheerness Fort, on the Kent side of the Thames. The fort's function was to guard the approaches to the River Medway but it was still under construction and its guns were not in service. In the face of a determined onslaught the defenders fled.

Dutch Ships guarding the Thames

On both the Essex and Kent sides of the River Thames locals were dumfounded to see the whole waterway filled with Dutch ships, able to raid at will and prevent any other shipping movement.

In London the Dutch incursion was at first dismissed as bravado. The Navy Board did nothing more than file reports and send letters to each other until news came that Sheerness Fort had been overrun. At this George Monck, who had previously been in sole charge of the admiralty, hurried east to inspect the defences. He found them 'pitiful'. Of the 800 men on the River Medway supposedly in the king's pay only a handful remained. Many small boats had disappeared too, taken by deserters desperate to escape. Meanwhile the Dutch were advancing along the Medway, contemptuously sweeping aside any opposition or obstacles put in their way. A heavy chain had been thrown across the Medway at Gillingham to block enemy ships entering but this had badly sagged and the Dutch ships sailed over it. The shore batteries proved ineffective and the situation seemed hopeless. Unfortunately George Monck, who was a very capable military leader, was accompanied by, in the words of Samuel Pepys, *a great many idle lords and gentlemen, with their pistols and fooleries.* These people were clueless in military matters and by issuing orders and countermanding them, made the situation infinitely worse.

For five days the Dutch remained in Chatham and in the process destroyed the *Royal James*, the *Loyal London*, the *Royal Oak* and several other capital ships. To add to the humiliation the Duke of York's flagship, the *Royal Charles,* was seized and towed back to Holland when they eventually departed.

For nearly the whole of July the Dutch controlled the River Thames. The English Navy was powerless. Fortunately the Chatham Dockyard was not destroyed which would have compounded the disaster. Luck was also with England when, on 4th July, an attack on Harwich by a powerful Dutch force failed after their flagship ran aground. Nevertheless, Dutch marines still stormed Landguard Fort in Suffolk on the other side of the River Stour, opposite Harwich. The Dutch withdrew, when unlike the defenders at Sheerness, the Landguard garrison fought back.

The authorities in London were in a state of panic. King Charles ordered peace negotiations to begin as soon as possible. By the 31st July agreement was reached and the second Anglo/Dutch war was over. A positive effect of this fiasco was that three years later Charles II commissioned the redesign and rebuilding of Tilbury fort.

A reminder of the Dutch attack in Essex is engraved on a stone tablet set into the wall of St Catherine's Parish Church, East Tilbury. It states that the original church tower and vicarage were destroyed during a naval battle on July 23rd 1667 at Tilbury Hope.

The third Anglo/Dutch war saw the Dutch blockade the Thames from time to time. However England had signed a secret peace treaty with the French who attacked Holland thus weakening their naval capabilities. The French invasion also sparked a rebellion in Holland during which Johan de Witt was murdered. Despite this the Dutch were able to send a fleet across the Atlantic and recapture New York. Hostilities continued sporadically until February 1674. This third war ended when King Charles signed the Treaty of Westminster. As part of the bargain New York was returned to the English Crown.

In East Tilbury. A reminder of the Dutch invasion

After the death of Charles, his brother James was crowned king in 1685. His reign was short and troubled and in the 'Glorious Revolution' of 1688 he was deposed. Then, ironically after all those wars with Holland, the Dutch grandson of Charles I, William of Orange, and his wife Mary, daughter of the deposed King James II, were invited to rule jointly as King William III and Queen Mary II of England and peace with Holland was assured.

THE KENT ARMADA
1724

Queen Anne, the last of the Stuart monarchs, passed away in 1714. She had succeeded her brother-in-law William III (of Orange) who had died following a riding accident. Anne was the first sovereign of Great Britain, as not only had the crowns of England and Scotland been united but so too had both parliaments in the Act of Union in 1707. Anne was succeeded by the 54 year old German Protestant, Prince George, Elector of Hanover, who ascended to the throne as George I.

In general, although the British were fighting various wars in continental Europe, there were no perceived threats to Great Britain as such. Internal trouble manifested itself in both Scotland and Ireland but England was relatively peaceful. However in the county of Essex the fishermen had other foes on their mind - the fishermen of Kent. Between them there was considerable animosity, more so than the fear of any 'foreign' invaders. The fishermen from Essex jealously viewed the successful oyster harvesting in and around Leigh-on-Sea and on the banks of Mersea Island on the River Blackwater. Numerous incidents were recorded of clashes with regard to fishing rights.

The most serious incident came in September 1724 when what was described as:-

'A fleet of a hundred fishing smacks from Kent, with flags waving, invaded the oyster beds of Leigh on Sea.' It was nicknamed the 'Kent Armada'. During the invasion 1,000 bushels (approximately twelve and a half tons) of oysters were plundered by the Kent men. Attempts by Leigh-on-Sea based fishermen to drive off the intruders were met with gunfire.

The extent of the Manor of Hadleigh, held by Westminster Abbey, stretched over the Leigh oyster beds. The manorial rights were administered by the tenants of Jarvis Hall and Hall Farm on behalf of the Dean and Chapter of Westminster; a body not to be trifled with. The raid, being in complete contravention of these rights, had its consequences. The Kent fishermen were brought to trial a year later at the Spring Assizes in Brentwood. The case was tried before Lord Chief Justice Baron Gilbert. Fourteen Kent men were found guilty of trespass and collectively fined over £2,000 (an enormous amount for the day).

Today oyster fishing is no longer undertaken in Leigh-on-Sea. In Essex, however, there is still a substantial industry based in and around West Mersea in the Blackwater estuary and in Colchester. The fishermen of Kent have their own oyster fishing based around Whitstable and as far as we know relations between Kent and Essex fishermen are now quite harmonious.

RAISING THE STANDARD

Gunpowder has played a decisive role in all battles since the late 16th century when muskets began to be used. Unfortunately it was not until the 18th century that consistency of quality was established. Prior to that date gunpowder in England was manufactured by a range of private companies whose primary aim was to make a profit. The national interest was secondary. Both the British Army and Navy were of the opinion that much of the gunpowder available was substandard; supply was inconsistent, with stocks running out when most needed, as happened during the Dutch wars and the American Revolutionary conflict.

Kept in a dark place. Gunpowder Barrels Ready for Shipment

To avoid the disaster of the American War recurring and with conflict with the French looming again, the British government decided to nationalise most of the private factories. In 1787, the Crown purchased the Essex Gunpowder Mills at Waltham Abbey in the Lea Valley from John Walton for £10,000 and thus the Royal Gunpowder Mills came into being. The site at Waltham Abbey was ideal, it was away from built up areas and was conveniently sited by the River Lea which enabled the finished product to be shipped by barge to the River Thames and then onwards to the military.

Under the watchful eye of Sir William Congreve, Deputy Comptroller of the Royal Laboratory at Woolwich Arsenal, new standards were set and rigorous quality control enforced. Manufacturing processes were upgraded to ensure continuous supply and substantial resources were allocated to research and development. The benchmarks of quality and cost established by the Royal Gunpowder mills were then imposed on the remaining gunpowder makers in the private sector. For over 200 years the mills remained under Government control with many innovations such as gun cotton, cordite, and the plastic explosive RDX being perfected there.

Although the primary purpose of the mills was to supply the military's needs it was also a catalyst in the advancement of explosives for civil use such as tunnelling, mining and quarrying. During the First World War over 6,000 people worked in the Waltham Abbey factories.

Production was dispersed during World War II for fear of enemy bombing. After the war the mills closed on 28th July 1945 only to reopen as the newly named, 'Explosives Research and Development Establishment'. In 1977 its name was changed again to the 'Propellants, Explosives and Rocket Motor Establishment', before being rebranded as the 'Royal Armament Research and Development Establishment'. This closed in 1991, bringing to an end over 200 years of explosives production and research at Waltham Abbey.

Currently the Royal Gunpowder Mills, using its original name, is an industrial heritage attraction and is open to the public at weekends and bank holidays throughout the spring and summer months.

DETERRING NAPOLEON
The Sea Fencibles and Martello Towers

King George III came to the throne in 1760. He was the third George of the house of Hanover, though the first to be born in England. Nicknamed 'Mad King George' due to his illnesses in later life, he ruled for 60 years. He is perhaps best remembered for his disastrous handling of the American Revolutionary War. He was the last British monarch to rule the thirteen colonies that became the United States of America. William Pitt the Younger, Britain's youngest Prime Minister at 24 years of age was in office from 1783 to 1801, a period of dynamic change in France.

Meanwhile across the channel the French revolution had produced a new and charismatic leader, Napoleon. He became the First Consul of the Republic in 1799 and later declared himself Emperor of all of France. His territorial ambitions throughout Europe alarmed the establishment in Great Britain who were already nervous of home grown revolutionaries inspired by events in France, where the people had overthrown the monarchy.

The Americans had gained their independence with strong support from the French, whose navy was increasing in size to rival that of the British. With Napoleon becoming ever more aggressive a seaborne invasion, mounted across the North Sea or the Channel seemed very real. This led to the creation of one of the least known military units in Great Britain, a coastal defence force known as the Sea Fencibles. This new force would cover the entire English coast facing the European mainland as well as Lands' End and the northern shoreline of Cornwall, Devon and Somerset up as far as Bristol.

The Sea Fencibles were a nautical Home Guard manned by part time volunteers. The Essex zone began in Leigh-on-Sea in the south of the county and ran around the Essex shoreline to Harwich. The force comprised about 1,500 men divided into small units, each serving their own community. Many of the volunteers lived in shacks on the coast and eked out a living from fishing and bait digging. One of the great advantages of joining the Sea Fencibles was that it exempted its members from being impressed into the navy. The fear of the navy's strong armed press gangs turning up unannounced was very real in coastal communities.

Many of the Fencibles lived around the Rivers Crouch, Blackwater and the Thames Estuary. They were probably involved in smuggling in one form or another and benefited enormously from the navy's distribution of weapons and offers of sea combat and signals training. As a bonus, they were also paid one shilling a day when they attended.

One of the Sea Fencibles most notable commanders was Sir Eliab Harvey, from the Rolls Park in Chigwell. He was appointed Captain of the Essex Fencibles while recovering from dengue fever contracted while in action in the West Indies. Harvey later went on to captain the *HMS Temeraire* and fought alongside Nelson at the Battle of Trafalgar.

The Fencibles were the nation's eyes and ears on the east coast and their duties included patrolling the coastline and reporting anything suspicious whilst assessing the coast in regard to its suitability for enemy landings. They were also charged with guarding the **Martello Towers.**

Guarding against the enemy. One of 29 built along the Essex and Suffolk Coast

Invaders were considered most likely to come ashore in the northern part of the county. The southern coastal area was marshy with many inlets unsuitable for landings while the forts on the Thames already protected the southern area.

From 1808 to 1812, twenty-nine Martello Towers were built between Aldeburgh in Suffolk and St Osyth Stone in Essex. Eleven of these were erected on the Essex coast between St Osyth Stone and Walton on the Naze backwaters. Their design and construction was inspired by the round fortress at Mortella Point in Corsica, built by the Genoese in the 1500s, that had withstood a determined seaborne siege.

The towers were circular in design to give good defence without blind spots. They contained living quarters, armoury, a kitchen and sufficient supplies of food, water and arms to resist an attack for lengthy periods. Their brick walls went from 2.4m (8ft) thick inland and up to 4m (13ft) thick on the seaward side. They stood up to 12m (40ft) in height and would have up to three cannon mounted on the roof.

In times of lower tension the towers were garrisoned by enough men to provide a 24 hour lookout. In the event of French forces being sighted all the towers could be reinforced from the reserve barracks close by at Weeley.

At the same time a supporting fort, the Redoubt, was built in Harwich in 1808. At its peak it had a garrison of 300 and its prime purpose was to protect the port. Built on top of a hill with a 70m (200ft) diameter, the Redoubt had clear views in all directions. Throughout its military life it was continually remodelled to keep up with gunnery technology, yet during 150 years of service not a shot was fired in anger. The Redoubt was given listed building status in 1969 and is the largest ancient monument in the UK. It is currently open as a museum.

As for the rest of the Martello Towers, by the time they were finished the victory at the battle of Trafalgar had made invasion less likely and their importance in the nation's defence faded. The Fencibles too were never called out to take part in any meaningful action. They were disbanded in 1810 and thereafter largely forgotten. Today six of the Essex Martello towers remain. Three are open to the public. Jaywick Tower is run as an arts centre but is open for visits, Clacton Marine Parade Tower is a small zoo and St Osyth Tower, at Point Clear, is an aviation museum.

SMALL ARMS

Just over two hundred years ago in 1812, when Napoleon was facing defeat in Russia, the Crown acquired an island between the channels of the River Lea to build an ordnance and small arms factory. The location was just south of the Waltham Abbey Gunpowder Mills (described from page 59). Until 1812, most weapons had been supplied from Birmingham's 'Gun Quarter' where small companies manufactured various components for other companies to assemble. These groups eventually came together to form BSA, the Birmingham Small Arms Company.

The marshy island chosen for the Royal Small Arms Factory (RSAF) in what is now Enfield was ideal. The site offered a degree of security. There was also water power to drive machinery and barges could transport raw materials from, and finished weapons to, sailing ships on the Thames. Completed in 1816, the factory gradually began to produce small arms. Even swords were made from 1823.

The RSAF pioneered the use in Britain of machinery for the production of interchangeable parts for small arms. The Crimean War in 1853 created a surge in demand, steam power was introduced and a new machine shop was built by the Royal Engineers. Production soared and by 1887 there were 2,400 employees.

Quite a community grew up around the factory with many of the workers living in purpose built cottages nearby. There was a school, a church, a fire brigade, eventually a police station and of course several public houses.

The RSAF became famous for its designs and none more so than the Lee Enfield Rifle designed by James Paris Lee in 1895. This rifle went into production four years later and, together with the Enfield Revolver, was to become the standard British Army issue for decades to come.

The advent of World War I brought further rapid expansion. The same thing happened in the build up to World War II. To cope with demand, Enfield designed weapons were also being manufactured at other sites less vulnerable to enemy bombing in this country and overseas, notably in Canada.

All weapons designed at the factory were identifiable by having the word Enfield or the letters EN in the name, for example the Bren, Sten and Tanden guns, among others.

Decline set in during the 1950s and by 1963 half the site was closed. The RSAF was decommissioned by the Ministry of Defence in 1984 and privatised as Royal Ordnance PLC. Closure was announced on 12th August 1987. The factory was later bought by British Aerospace (BAe) and all the machinery and equipment auctioned off the following year. BAe then developed the site creating an attractive urban village. Adjacent to the village is Gunpowder Park (in Essex), an area that was once used as a testing ground for ordnance and explosives.

In 2010 a barge was moored in the millpond in front of the historic RSAF workshops as a heritage feature. As far as it is known the barge was never used for RSAF purposes, formerly being the *Fairview*, a disused narrow boat. Following a makeover the barge was given a new name, *Harold Turpin*, the co-inventor of the sten gun.

CAPTAIN SWING

In June 1830, William IV ascended to the throne aged 69. He was the third son of 'Mad King George' and the last of the Hanoverian kings. Arthur Wellesley, the Duke of Wellington, was prime minister but what greatness he had displayed on the battlefield didn't follow him into politics. Wellesley's great triumphs in the Napoleonic wars were over. Many soldiers and sailors had returned home from years of service overseas only to swell the ranks of the unemployed and to face a life of destitution in an ungrateful nation. To add to their woes the country was suffering from shortages due to a succession of terrible harvests.

The enclosure acts of 1773 to 1801 had seen the demise of the small tenant farmer and the disappearance of common lands, leaving agricultural labourers forced to work for the large landowners on ever decreasing wages. Then, with the industrial revolution, came mechanisation. The introduction of threshing machines deprived men of the work they once relied upon in the winter months. The levels of hardship grew until, in 1830, much of rural southeast England and East Anglia was engulfed in a great wave of protest machine breaking. All the while the Prime Minister seemed indifferent to the plight of the men who had served him so loyally on the battlefield.

Machines: The Target for Captain Swing

Things came to a head in Essex on 7th December when a mob of 150 ran riot in Great Clacton and caused a great deal of property damage. Two days later a similar sized group assembled in the dead of night in Little Clacton with the express purpose of destroying a threshing machine kept in a locked barn there. Demonstrations and acts of vandalism also happened simultaneously throughout the Tendring Hundred.

At Kirby the crowd had been estimated at 300. In Great Holland 100 men had gathered; 140 at Little Clacton; 150 in the village of Tendring and 200 at Ramsey. The protests were characterised by there being no attacks on persons, only on the hated machines. Nevertheless rebellion on this scale called for strong counter measures.

The anonymous leader of the rioters was a *'Captain Swing'* who supposedly took his name from the 'swing' or moving part of the flail used to thresh the grain. The protests became known the *Swing Riots*. After the unrest died down, the authorities showed little mercy in pursuing the rioters. Fifty men from Clacton were charged with a variety of offences. Nationally some 2,000 men and women were convicted and over 500 were transported to Van Diemen's Land (modern day Tasmania) to serve between 5 and 14 year terms.

One local man, Benjamin Hackshall, escaped arrest by hiding up a neighbour's chimney. He then fled to London where he was apprehended by a 'Bow Street Runner'*. Luckily he escaped transportation. After serving a relatively short spell in Chelmsford jail, he returned to his family in Little Clacton. Hackshall then became a minor celebrity by composing a popular ballad which gave a romantic account of the riots. Five years later, 200 of those transported received free pardons.

The Duke of Wellington was vehemently opposed to any reform of parliament and the voting system and appeared to have little sympathy with the post war hardships. Many viewed him as a reactionary. With parliament divided or deadlocked and the country beset by civil unrest, his tenure as Prime Minister was abruptly terminated on November 15th 1830, when a combination of reformers and vengeful opponents defeated him in a vote.

The Bow Street Runners were so called because they were based at Bow Street magistrates' court in London. As they didn't wear uniforms they were considered the forerunners of the modern day CID (Criminal Investigation Department).

PALMERSTON'S FOLLIES

In 1860, Queen Victoria was enjoying the 23rd year of her reign. In response to concerns about the strength of the French Navy, a Royal Commission recommended the building of a series of forts around the British coastline to defend what were classed as 'key' areas. They were named after the Prime Minister of the day, Lord Palmerston (Henry John Temple) as the Palmerston Forts.

From their inception there was vigorous debate in parliament as to whether the costs could be justified. Nevertheless with the strong backing of the Prime Minster, the project went ahead to become the most costly and extensive system of fixed defences undertaken in peacetime.

Over 30 forts and defence structures were built from scratch or on top of existing fortifications, including Coalhouse Fort near Tilbury and Beacon Hill at Harwich. Coalhouse Fort was built in its present form on the site of existing gun batteries and was supervised by Colonel Charles George Gordon (of Khartoum). It took 14 years to complete, by which time the chief promoter of the scheme, Lord Palmerston, had been dead for nine years. The finished fort had walls five feet thick. The roofs, made of brick and concrete, were also protected by granite and iron shields. Yet by the time the fort was ready, the rapidly changing technology of gunnery and munitions had rendered it obsolete. Practice firings had to be kept to a minimum as the shock waves broke windows in Tilbury and Gravesend. The casemated heavy-duty structure of the fort restricted the angle of firing or the replacement of the guns with newer ones. The life of a gunner was particularly miserable too, due to the deafening noise and choking black smoke in the confines of the casemate.

The forts soon acquired the name *Palmerston's Follies*, in part because the defences constructed around Portsmouth had their main guns facing inland to protect the city from a land-based attack rather than anything from the sea. All the while the forts were considered to be of questionable military value. Even during its active service, the artillery within Coalhouse Fort never once fired a defensive shot in anger. Only in the Second World War (80 years after it had been planned) did that change when operational anti-aircraft guns were placed on the roof.

Coalhouse Fort today is considered to be one of the finest

Coalhouse Fort:
Walls five foot thick but
in 90 years, not a shot fired in anger

examples of an armoured casemated fort in the United Kingdom. After being decommissioned in 1949, it was leased, to be used as a storage facility by the Bata shoe factory of East Tilbury.

It was purchased in 1962 by Thurrock Council who, after creating a riverside park of the surroundings, leased it in 1983 to the 'Coalhouse Fort Project', a heritage charity operated by volunteers.

Despite the lack of combat action Coalhouse Fort and its adjacent artillery defences were collectively designated a scheduled monument in recognition of their status as 'a remarkable group of defensive sites'.

THIRD CHOICE

In 1849, the British Government, through the Board of Ordnance (the body responsible for supplying munitions to the military) purchased land at Shoeburyness to test artillery. The negotiations were protracted and took the best part of five years to complete. At that time the nation's principal gunnery range was on Plumstead Marshes, on the south bank of the River Thames near Woolwich, where test firings were arranged in such a way that the line of fire went over the river. In the 1840s the River Thames was an increasingly busy waterway. Nearly all the vessels serving the capital were powered by sail so passage was slow and subject to the tide. Accordingly test firings were frequently interrupted or abandoned because of the danger to shipping. This situation was most unsatisfactory and a parliamentary select committee instructed the Board of Ordnance to look for a new site.

A location near Sandwich in Kent was short listed but the local landowner, Lord Guildford, rejected the proposal out of hand. He wrote to say, 'It would a ruinous invasion on the most valuable part of my property'. After a half-hearted legal challenge the Solicitor General advised the board to give up on Kent. The next choice was an area close to Landguard Fort in Suffolk, just across the Orwell estuary from Harwich. Again the local landowner, the Duke of Hamilton, objected. He was planning to build a seaside resort known as the 'The Place' and argued that an artillery range close by would devalue and destroy his project. Once again the Board of Ordnance withdrew. Over the course of time 'The Place' became the town of Felixstowe.

In contrast to these rebuffs the board received an offer of a site from the Parish of South Shoebury. An initial evaluation from inspectors produced a favourable report. However, although there was a coast guard station at Shoeburyness, the main drawback was its remoteness. Roads were poor, access from the sea erratic because of the tides and the railway was yet to come.

Ministry inspectors and surveyors carried out more feasibility studies, talked to local landowners and heard objections. One of these, although it is not clear who raised it, was that the proposed artillery range and barracks would occupy a former Viking encampment. It also seems that some of the senior military officers were very reluctant to commit to Shoeburyness. They considered the location far too inhospitable for them and their officials in the winter months. Nevertheless the pressure to test weapons and ammunition was mounting and, despite ongoing negotiations, the army began preparing the site during the summer and autumn of 1849. During the following year what were known as 'Mr Hale's 'stickless' rockets' were first tested.

Work stopped abruptly with the onset of winter and the troops returned to Woolwich. Over the next four years some firing platforms were installed, the ranges marked out, wooden accommodation huts were built and a makeshift hospital created. Yet the work parties only came in spring and then left in the autumn. It was known as 'the season'. Apparently the Essex winters were proving a 'little too hard' for the soldiers and their officers.

All this time the Board of Ordnance considered Shoeburyness as a stop gap. It held a tight grip on the purse strings, blocking finance to build proper accommodation or even secure storage for fuel (coal or wood was prone to pilfering). As a consequence many of the men had to live in tents. The catering facilities were poor and sanitation appalling. Eventually, and grudgingly, it was agreed that Shoeburyness should become a permanent station, but it was not until the Crimean War broke out in 1854 that development of the Shoebury ranges began in earnest. The British Army had not fought a major war since the Battle of Waterloo 40 years earlier. Mobilization for Crimea found the military dysfunctional at all levels and the Shoebury development was one of the urgent steps taken to rectify this.

What would later be known as the 'Old Ranges' at Shoeburyness underwent a major expansion. With the coming of new breech loading guns and ordinance the first British School of Gunnery was established in 1859. However there were always dangers. In February 1885 the detonation of a 6in shell resulted in seven deaths which included that of the Commandant. Four of these were buried at St Andrews Church, Shoebury.

Further expansion followed in 1890 with the acquisition of the 'New Ranges' on Foulness Island. The establishment was at its peak during the First World War. In 1915 an anti-aircraft school of instruction was formed and in 1917, Lieutenant-Colonel Edwin Richardson started the British War Dog School. During World War II an anti-tank training unit came into being. After the Second World War the 'Old Ranges' at Shoeburyness contracted rapidly. Specialist units were disbanded or moved to other parts of the country.

Big Guns on the Shoebury Ranges c1883

The garrison HQ closed in 1976. Today some of its brick built structures have been preserved, with listed status within a conservation area. The rest of the site was then sold for housing development as 'The Shoebury Garrison' estate.

On Foulness the 'New Ranges' continued in various incarnations, although doing much the same as they had always done in terms of weapons and armaments testing and development In 1920, the site became known as the Experimental Establishment (XP) and in 1948 it was renamed the Proof and Experimental Establishment (P&EE) before becoming the Land and Maritime Ranges. This changed again in 2001 when all the military staff left and weapons' testing was outsourced to a private defence contractor.

KYNOCHTOWN

Whilst the Shoebury Ranges were being built up under direct control of the military, there were still a few private companies operating outside the semi-nationalised gunpowder industry.

In 1897, with the second Boer war looming, Kynoch and Company Ltd, a Birmingham based munitions manufacturer, were looking to expand. They chose the peninsula of Shell Haven on the marshy Essex shore of the Thames, next to Canvey Island, to build an explosives factory. The extra capacity would help to cope with their expected upsurge in demand for munitions.

A new village of Kynochtown was built to accommodate the workforce, originally consisting of forty houses, a school and a shop that also served as a post office. It was called Shell Haven after the shell bar in one of the creeks by Canvey Island. Although the site would become a major oil terminal and refinery many years later, there is no connection with the giant Shell oil company of today.

The company prospered and although there was a constant danger from air raids during the First World War, the manufacture of explosives continued until 1919. It ceased then, ostensibly due to the risk of flooding, but a more likely reason would seem to be a downturn in demand once the war was over. Although the factory closed, the village of Kynochtown remained.

Four years later construction began on an oil refinery for the Cardiff based Cory brothers and the village was renamed Coryton. Oil refining stopped during WW2 but continued post war under 'Mobil Oil'. As the industrial site grew the wisdom of having housing in the middle of such a potentially dangerous complex was questioned.

During the 1960s, in the interests of safety, all the villagers were gradually re-housed in Corringham and by 1974 the original village had been demolished. In 1900 the Kynoch company had also built a hotel on Canvey Island, the 'Kynoch Hotel', which survived to accommodate military personnel during the Second World War. It too was demolished in 1960 and the name Kynochtown passed into history.

The Kynock Hotel on Canvey Island
– accessed only by boat from Kynochtown
Once a desirable place to stay

THE FIRST WORLD WAR
1914 - 1918

Just remember
this was a time when there
was no radio, no television,
no internet or social media,
there were few telephones
and photography
and film were in
their infancy.

If you **could not** read you had to
rely on word of mouth to get the
news.

THE GREAT WAR

Queen Victoria died in January 1901. Her successor was her eldest son, 59 year old Edward VII.

In, general, as the 19th century turned into the 20th century, although Essex and the country at large were generally peaceful, British forces were engaged in a bitter war against the Boers in South Africa. The relief of Mafeking in May 1900, where the British were under siege for 217 days, was a turning point in the war. In Rochford a huge bonfire, lit to celebrate this event, got out of control and a near riot ensued. 'Hooligans' commandeered several delivery carts, broke them up to add to the blaze. Police tried to intervene but they were chased away. Although hardly a battle this was symptomatic of the feelings of relief across the country.

1910 was marked by two General Elections, the first in January and the second in December. Both resulted in the formation of a coalition government. The December election was quite rowdy. When Winston Churchill visited Colchester in late November in support of the local Liberal candidate he was pelted with eggs and rotten fish. Later in the evening the rival party campaign headquarters was attacked and a number of shops torched.

Also in 1910 George V, Edward's second son, ascended to the throne following the death of his father. George's reign was marked by the rise of Irish republicanism, socialism, communism and fascism, the Indian independence movement and also by the limited voting franchise being extended to women. Yet between 1914 and 1918 the nation's affairs were dominated by the Great, or First World War.

Unlike other conflicts, the First World War didn't bring any worries of 'foreign' invasion to begin with. When war was declared in August 1914, life in Essex carried on much as usual, after all the official view was that the war would be over by Christmas. In fact the resorts of Southend-on-Sea and Clacton placed large display advertisements in the London newspapers appealing for holidaymakers to continue to come 'as all the entertainments are open for business as usual', (see opposite).

Following appeals from Lord Kitchener, hundreds of thousands of men volunteered to join up and continued to do so, despite 57,000 British casualties being reported by early November. There was also a hunt to find 'aliens'. Germans or Austrians living in the country were targeted especially; they were considered potential spies or saboteurs.

BUSINESS AS USUAL

SOUTHEND'S MOTTO

" BUSINESS AS USUAL."

EVERY AMUSEMENT UNDER THE SUN CAN BE FOUND IN

THE KURSAAL & GARDENS

The whole of the 18 Acres of Gardens and miles of Attractions

Remain Open Daily till September 30th.

NO ONE SHOULD LEAVE SOUTHEND WITHOUT PAYING A VISIT.

SOUTHEND'S MOTTO

"BUSINESS AS USUAL."

The *Woodford Times* reported the case of an English woman, Alice Lergenmuller, aged 45, of Whitney Road, Leyton being brought before Stratford Magistrates charged with being an enemy alien who had failed to register herself. Mrs Lergenmuller had married a German in 1904 but he had deserted her one year into the marriage. She had gone to Leyton Police station to tell them of her circumstances; however, the police arrested her, then later released her and told her to register as an alien. In Southend, Elizabeth Schmidt and Edith Gretineau were charged with being aliens. Both were married to Swiss nationals and didn't believe they needed to register. Ignorance of the law was deemed no excuse. Both women were told to register and no further action would be taken if the court costs were paid.

Despite the outward normality, all munitions factories ramped up production and 1915 brought with it the realisation that the war, which had not ended by the previous Christmas as hoped, was unlikely to end in the near future. The Essex Farmers Union wondered how the crops would be harvested with so many agricultural workers joining the military.

ZEPPELINS

War from the air hit Essex with the Zeppelin raids. During the night of 15/16th April 1915 these German airships struck Maldon and in May they targeted Southend where over 100 bombs were dropped. One person was killed, several were injured and there was extensive property damage. In May and July Barking and East Ham were also bombed, sparking riots and looting in Southend, Grays and across East London. Many commercial premises, thought to be owned by families of German or Austrian origin, were targeted. Hundreds of people, many them intoxicated, attacked the premises of Messrs Glasson's furniture dealers in Grays only to discover later that Mr Glasson was an English man.

The Zeppelin raids continued throughout 1915 and there seemed no means of stopping them. However, with the improvement in anti-craft guns and better fighter aircraft, home forces gradually neutralised the threat from the Zeppelins. Two incidents in Essex bear witness to this. On the 23rd – 24th September 1916, the German navy launched a twelve Zeppelin raid on England. Four of these were the latest 'Super Airships' and targeted London. One, code named L30, dropped its bombs at sea, failing even to make the coast, whilst another, L31, approached from the south, crossed the Thames and bombed Leyton, killing eight people and injuring thirty. The two other Zeppelins, whilst trying to make it back to their home bases, came to a sticky end in Essex. L32 was attacked over Purfleet at about 1:00am by a Royal Flying Corps BE2c fighter and set alight. It crashed in flames near Great Burstead. There were no survivors.

The last of the four, L33, after dropping bombs on Bromley-by-Bow and Upminster, turned for home across Essex. It was hit by anti-aircraft fire as well as being damaged by night fighters from RAF Hainault. Losing height, L33 headed toward the coast where Captain Alois Böcker, who was on his first mission, ordered the jettisoning of guns and equipment in a desperate attempt to maintain height. Having just managed to limp across the Essex coast he realised that he would not make it home. He turned his ship back towards Mersea Island. The Zeppelin eventually made a forced, but safe, landing near New Hall Farm in Little Wigborough in the small hours of the morning. All the crew were able to scramble out. Before destroying his airship by setting fire to it,

Captain Böcker approached local cottages in an attempt to warn local residents. The terrified occupants, however, did not open their doors. With the airship burning fiercely the Germans marched off in the direction of Colchester only to be stopped by Special Constable Edgar Nicholas who was cycling to investigate the blaze. Nicholas accompanied them to Peldon Post Office where they were formally arrested by PC 354, Charles Smith.

Peldon did not have a Police Station and the enemy crew, much to the disquiet of local residents was put up overnight in the parish hall. The following day the 'prisoners' were escorted to Mersea Island where they were formally taken into custody by the military. The Chief Constable, on hearing the news of his prompt action, promoted PC Smith to the rank of Sergeant. Until he died, at the age of 94, he was known by all as 'Zepp' Smith.

The burnt out airship provided the British with much information about the Zeppelins' construction, which was used in the design of the later British R33-class airships.

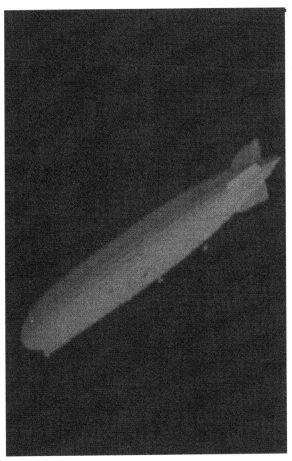

L33's doomed flight

79

THE EARLY AIRFIELDS

Essex had been at the forefront of aircraft development since the first aerodrome and testing ground was built at Dagenham in January 1909. At the onset of WW1 in August 1914 the government, rightly assuming that London would be the primary target for German aircraft, decided that East Anglia and Kent were where air defences should be developed.

In 1915, the London Air Defence Area (LADA) was established. The construction of a number of airfields quickly followed. Seaplanes, already based at Clacton, were charged with regularly patrolling the Thames Estuary to spot enemy planes or airships. These were the first military aircraft based in Essex. Eight landing grounds were rapidly established with the primary aim of protecting London's eastern approaches. In 1916 North Weald and Stow Maries airfields were commissioned and several other sites (no more than just fields) were requisitioned for emergency landing; necessary since the early planes had a propensity to run out of fuel or develop engine troubles.

The 90 acre Sutton's Farm airfield in South Hornchurch, 14 miles from central London and close to the Thames, was ideally placed to guard against German airships that used the river as a navigation aid. It was from Sutton's Farm that Lt. William Leefe Robinson achieved fame by shooting down Zeppelin SL11 on 2nd September 1916. He was awarded the Victoria Cross for this achievement and was feted as a national hero. His success was very quickly followed by that of two more pilots from Hornchurch; Lt. Frederick Sowrey for his part in the destruction of Zeppelin L32, which came down in flames at Great Burstead, near Billericay, and Lt. Wulstan Tempest who shot down Zeppelin L31 over Potters Bar in October 1916. Both pilots were awarded the DSO for their part in the destruction of these once seen as impregnable airships. Many streets in South Hornchurch are named after these and other pilots of WW1.

Hainault Farm landing site was formed in early 1915 on land requisitioned from the farm of that name to the west of Romford. From April to August it housed the Home Defence, No 39 squadron, consisting of three flights; A, B and C. C was based at Hainault but the other two were located at satellite stations, A at North Weald and B at Sutton's Farm, Hornchurch. Later, in 1917, these flights would form the core of Home Defence No. 44 Squadron which stayed at Hainault throughout the rest of the war.

Squadron 37 was the other Home Defence squadron operational in Essex during 1916. With headquarters in Woodham Mortimer its A flight was based at Rochford, B flight at Stow Maries and C flight based at Goldhanger. It was from Goldhanger's C flight that, on 17th June 1917, Lt. Watkins engaged the last Zeppelin to be shot down in England during the war.

Soon after peace was declared, in 1919, most of the airfields and landing grounds were closed and the land reverted to its pre-war owners, some becoming private airfields for flying clubs. However Stow Maries, near present day South Woodham Ferrers, is considered to be the only surviving World War I aerodrome in Europe. It operates as a charitable trust supported by English Heritage.

The largest of the Home Defence stations of WW1 was Rochford. Its role as a night fighter station came to an end in 1919 and the station closed a year later. The site was brought back into service in 1935 when Southend Municipal Airport was opened. Southend Council sold the airport to the Stobart Group in 2008 since when, after many improvements, it has become 'London Southend Airport'.

****

On 5th January 1916 the '**COMPULSION BILL**' (Conscription) cleared its first reading in the House of Commons with a majority of 298. With over 300,000 casualties to date, including 50,000 dead and a further 50,000 classed as missing, the army could no longer rely on volunteers to fill its needs.

Yet, despite the war, on 1st September 1916 Southend enthusiastically reported 'house full' in August. The families of munitions workers had come to Southend in vast numbers and had vied with each other to pay higher and higher prices for lodgings in the town.

A man who will not help his country is helping the enemy.

**Prove you are willing to help.
Enrol now for National Service.**

Forms can be obtained from any Post Office, National Service Office, or Employment Exchange. Fill up one without delay.

from the Essex County Chronicle

The 'Great Advance' (The Battle of the Somme) which was glowingly reported during the previous July and August had come to an end by November. Very little was reported in the press at the time.

The advance had gained about six miles (10 kilometres) at a cost of over 400,000 British casualties. January 1917 saw little in the way of definitive 'war news'. The optimistic reports that had appeared in the papers at the beginning of 1915 and 1916 were absent.

The *Southend Standard* summed up the situation on 18th January 1917 in an editorial that read, 'Although the official communiques give little indication beyond artillery fire, the list of casualties suggests that trench warfare is being conducted with concentrated energy. It is not a case of conquering territory; it is a test of endurance'.

Later, in contrast, the Colchester based *Essex County Telegraph* optimistically reported cheering news from the battle front of a great victory at Arras with over 12,000 prisoners and 150 guns taken. The report concluded that the enemy army was no longer invincible and the foe completely demoralised.

THE BIG BANG

The military were in crisis over a severe shortage of reliable high explosives. History was repeating itself; 200 years earlier the government had acquired the Gunpowder Mills at Waltham Abbey to solve a similar crisis. This time the Brunner Mond Company came to the rescue and their Silvertown factory, that had originally opened in 1894 but was standing idle, was reopened and rapidly adapted for the purification of the high explosive Trinitrotoluene or T.N.T.

The newly established Ministry of Munitions was charged with improving the supply and quantity of high explosives. Until 1915 the purification of T.N.T had been regarded as relatively safe though little was known about the methods of purifying it on a large scale. However it was recognised that the purification of T.N.T was far more dangerous than its actual manufacture. The Ministry therefore deemed that purification should be carried out in separate, and preferably isolated, factories. Despite these recommendations and the objections of the management, Lord Moulton, the Director-General of the Explosives Department, persuaded Brunner Mond to begin T.N.T purification at Silvertown.

The parish of West Ham, which Silvertown was part of, was developing rapidly. Hundreds of factories had been established, taking advantage of the less stringent planning regulations in Essex. With the factories came the workers and West Ham's population soared. By 1915 the Brunner Mond factory was in one of the most densely populated areas of the country.

For two years purification of T.N.T proceeded without incident. On 19th January, 1917 work at the factory went on as normal. Ten hour shifts were producing nine tons of explosive per day. Sometime around 5pm a small fire broke out near a loading hoist. The fire brigade was called and attempted to extinguish the blaze. Then at 6.51pm a devastating explosion ripped through the plant and at 6.52pm the chemical works were no more. The *Stratford Express* described the scene;

"The whole heavens were lit in awful splendour. A fiery glow seemed to have come over the dark and miserable January evening, and objects which a few minutes before had been blotted out in the intense darkness were silhouetted against the sky."

The blast destroyed hundreds of properties in the immediate area with many thousands more damaged to some degree. A large plywood factory, a flour mill and 17 acres of warehouses in the docks were among those severely damaged. The explosion was heard 100 miles away. The blast also caused a gas-holder on the Greenwich Peninsula to explode releasing eight million cubic feet of gas in a huge fireball. The Silvertown Fire Station, which had been completed three years earlier, was destroyed along with the firemen's houses.

Sixty-nine people were killed outright in the explosion including Dr Andreas Angel, the plant's chief chemist, who was helping to put out the original fire.

ESCAPE

Increasing numbers of enemy prisoners of war were being brought back to England. Many came to Essex and were put to work on farms which helped alleviate the labour shortage as so many English farm hands had left the land and were serving with the forces. However not all enemy prisoners were considered 'low risk' and some were locked up as they were considered to be dangerous or potential escapees. Although escapes were rare they were not unheard of.

On June 1st 1917, it was reported that Lieutenant Otto Thalen, of the German Army, and Lieutenant Lehman, of the German Navy - said to be a 'U-boat' officer, had broken out of Chelmsford detention barracks.

Lieut. Thalen was notorious for his attempts at prison breaking. In September 1915, with another officer, he had escaped from Donnington Hall (in Derbyshire) by digging a tunnel under the outer wall. They succeeded in getting to sea, but were caught on the way to Copenhagen by a British patrol boat. In February 1916, Thalen tried to escape from a Maidenhead camp by sawing through the floor of their hut, while his companion played a mouth organ to deaden the sound.

Lieut. Lehman, three months previously, had escaped from the custody of the military police at Manchester railway station. He was caught two days later in a Staffordshire village and charged with sacrilege after breaking into a Methodist chapel and making a fire of some bibles.

On this occasion these two were safely incarcerated in separate cells in Chelmsford. They were checked at 7 o'clock on Saturday night the

26th May yet at a quarter to eight on Sunday morning their cells were empty.

The escape demonstrated ingenuity and careful planning on the part of the prisoners. The cell doors posed no problem. They had loosened the screws attaching the locks making them removable at will and disguised their work with fake, blackened cardboard, covers. The cells were inspected, through peep holes in the door, periodically throughout the night. The sentries were deceived however by dummy figures, with realistic looking hair, lying in the beds. Having left their cells there were more obstacles. The iron gates to exit the building and the doors through the outer walls would require keys. There was a well-equipped workshop in the prison and one of the prisoners who had had mechanical training was alleged to have made a set duplicate keys.

Once the escape was discovered a hue and cry was raised and a search begun. The Military, the Essex Constabulary and Special Constables collaborated, with parties in motor cars, on cycles and afoot scouring the countryside. Although the fugitives managed to get out of the prison, their planning for what do outside was less comprehensive and within 24 hours the fugitives were recaptured by a cyclist corps near Basildon. The crisis was over and the citizens of Essex could sleep easy at night!

DEATH FROM THE SKIES

After a brief period of being free from bombing from Zeppelins, the war hit Essex with a vengeance on 12th August 1917 when Gotha bombers struck Southend-on-Sea. The raid took place just after 5pm, when visitors and residents were leaving the beaches. The bombing resulted in the deaths of 32 people (including 9 children) and injures to a further 50. The greatest numbers were killed by a bomb falling on Victoria Avenue, close to the train station which was thronged with day trippers waiting to take their train home. There was also widespread property damage throughout the town.

The subsequent rescue operation was hampered by visitors who immediately turned into sightseers and relic hunters, despite the best efforts of the police to move them on.

QUESTIONS THAT WILL BE ASKED BY THE CHILDREN

What did you do in the great big war?
Oh, tell me, daddy dear!
Did you quickly answer your country's call
And join as a Volunteer?
Or were you one of the men that was pressed
To fight the common foe?

Yes my child I fought in the great big war
For Freedom and all that is right.
I fought from the first as a Volunteer
And fought with all my might.
I thought of your mother, and you, and home
And all that a man holds dear.
See, here are the scars of the honourable wounds
In a fight which I had no fear.

I'm glad to hear you say dear dad,
That you fought in the great big war.
For when asked for what part you took
I shall hesitate no more
To tell my friends of your wounds
From shot and shell: midst death and swoone,
Of brave men, in agony,
And when you're called to final rest,
I'll think of you dad amongst the blest,
With honourable men who passed the test.

*Sent to the Grays and Tilbury Gazette by
Mr A. R. Ayling of North Hill,
Colchester a patient in the Orsett
Isolation Hospital.
Published 15/09/1917.*

MILITARY TRIBUNALS

The Military Tribunals that were established following the introduction of conscription had plenty of work to do. Their job was to determine whether requests for exemption from the call up had any merit.

Requests for exemption came from individual males but frequently it was from their employer. They pleaded that if their employee was called up, the business would suffer or even close. Sometimes requests for call up to be deferred came from distraught parents. In September the *Essex Weekly News* reported a case under the headline **THE LAST SON**. An unnamed widow from Burnham had pleaded with the tribunal that her youngest and seventh son should be exempt from overseas military service. The case was referred to the Essex County Tribunal. The mother explained that the son in question had already signed up and was training machine gunners. She said that he was already, 'Doing his bit'. She added that his six brothers had already joined. One had since been killed, another maimed and another was very ill. The mother asked if this son could be left in England, as she feared she might lose them all. However, the request was declined.

THE LAST YEAR OF WAR

1917 had seen the establishment of Food Control Committees and the introduction of food rationing, ration cards and price controls. In 1918 the rationing became more severe, price controls more exacting and the Food Control Committees more authoritarian. There was even a shortage of newsprint!

As the year progressed there was generally optimistic 'war' news to report, although shortages at home became more acute and included basic foodstuffs and also coal. In September 1918 there was a bout of strikes which affected coal production, the railways and the docks. Workers at the Co-operative Wholesale Factory in Silvertown also walked out, halting the distribution of cotton products.

The armistice came into effect on Monday 11th November 1918 at 11.00am. The guns fell silent and killing stopped. The *Essex Times* reported widespread celebrations throughout the county to mark the end of the war and, more amazingly, it informed its readers that as far as West

Ham Magistrates court was concerned, not one single case of drunkenness, assault or any ordinary crime was brought to court in that week.

THE UNSEEN ENEMY

Although the fighting in Europe ended, a new and deadly foe had become established on the home front. It was unseen, advancing rapidly and taking no prisoners.

Influenza was rampant and deadly. It struck the young and the old without mercy. No area of the county, whether built-up or rural, escaped as the virus attacked with equal ferocity. Countywide, schools were closed. In Manor Park cemetery, 53 bodies lay in the chapel awaiting burial. The army was called in to dig graves in Ilford. The Mayor of East Ham appealed to the local tribunal for any military call ups in process for undertakers or their assistants to be deferred. The War Office responded by sending a team of carpenters to make extra coffins. At Saffron Walden Prisoner of War Camp, Captain Gort the commandant died suddenly after becoming infected and of the 90 prisoners, 50 were ill. In Southend-on-Sea, crowds besieged the Ministry of Food Offices. With so many staff off sick the issue of new ration books had been suspended.

The Undertakers Cart –
A feared sight in the county

Dr J. C. Thresh, the Medical Officer of Heath for the county, released a statement which was read on the steps of County Hall.

'The epidemic is very bad, but we have it under control. We have an idea it follows the railways, especially the lines from London to Colchester, Southend and Cambridge. We believe it spreads because of overcrowded railway carriages. Many people have succumbed within 24 hours of their journey. Influenza is conveyed person to person. Every time a man or woman coughs, sneezes or exhales a variety of invisible bacteria is released.'

The influenza epidemic of 1918-1920 was one the deadliest natural disasters in human history. The death toll was estimated to have been between 20 million and 50 million victims worldwide with as many as 250,000 in the UK alone. Unfortunately the exact numbers are impossible to know due to a lack of medical record-keeping in many places. Exactly where it started was difficult to pinpoint and why it abated is subject to numerous theories as there was no magic drug suddenly made available to cure it.

As the war ended the pioneering medical photographer and journalist Norman K. Harrison from Clacton wrote that there was an urgent need to build 400,000 houses. He said 'There was no problem of more vital importance to the nation than that of housing.' He continued 'housing affects all areas of life such as health, child welfare, happiness and industrial efficiency'. He summarised the appalling housing conditions he had encountered and the degrading effects it had on the people living in them with the sad tale of a Mrs Simms who lived in a damp, filthy two roomed house with her five small children and another eight occupants. 'One morning Mrs Simms awoke, coughed and then died. Her children looked on wide eyed and wondered what to do. Mrs Simms had no insurance and no savings'.

Mr Harrison wondered what would become of the children and who next would move into the house? He urged the government, now the war was over, to put in a massive programme of house building, but said that although there had been encouraging noises from Ministers, he was of the opinion that he was 'flogging a dead horse'. He concluded by saying no matter what the crisis, 'The British capacity for muddling through is enormous and will be needed in the chaos to come'.

THE BATTLE OF THE FLAGS

Although the First World War had come to an end the nation faced severe problems. Despite the influenza epidemic abating, pockets of it persisted in certain areas and much of the blame was put on sub-standard housing.

The Prime Minister, David Lloyd George, perhaps heeding the advice of Norman Harrison promised to make Britain 'a place fit for heroes to live in'. In response the London County Council (LCC) took up the challenge and embarked on a plan to turn the slogan 'Homes for Heroes' into reality. In 1921 the LCC purchased the Valence Estate in Dagenham to build what was to become the biggest public housing development in the world, 'The Becontree Estate'. Within eleven years, over 20,000 houses were built and became home to a population of some 100,000 people.

Meanwhile two international developments, the Russian Revolution and Irish Independence, had had a profound effect in mid-Essex. It is difficult to imagine Thaxted, located midway between Great Dunmow and Saffron Walden in the rural countryside of Essex, as a hotbed of social unrest. Yet, Conrad Le Dispenser Noel, the Vicar of the parish church, began a chain of events that transformed the town into a political maelstrom. Between May and July 1921 mobs of up to 3,000 descended upon Thaxted on at least five occasions intent on removing the flags and banners the vicar had put up in the church. There were numerous disturbances in the streets with running fist-fights and even gun shots. It became known as the *Battle of the Flags*. Conrad Noel acquired the name of 'The Red Vicar' and the mobs were led in the main by undergraduates from Cambridge University.

Conrad Noel was born in 1869 in Kew, London. From an early age he showed a rebellious streak, he described his life in public school as incarceration. He went on to Corpus Christi College, Cambridge where, after being suspended for his radical socialist beliefs, he dropped out and failed to complete his degree. After training at Chichester Theological College, he was refused ordination into the Church of England, again because of his political beliefs. A curacy at All Saints Church in Plymouth was offered, but Noel was unacceptable to the Bishop of Exeter. Finally, at the age of 25, he was ordained Deacon in the Diocese of Chester before, in 1904, becoming an assistant priest at Primrose Hill in London. Two years later, with others, Noel formed the Church Socialist League. He was a founding member of the British Socialist Party but left to found the Catholic Crusade to propagate his views.

Conrad Noel arrived in Essex in 1910 to take up his appointment as the Vicar of Thaxted. His great patron was the eccentric, socialist Countess of Warwick, Daisy Greville, of Easton Lodge, one of the grandest of Essex estates, near Great Dunmow.

The end of the First World War brought a great number of issues to a head. Noel was incensed at the great divide between the wealthy and the poor in Britain. Irish independence was becoming a reality and the czarist regime in Russia had been overthrown by revolution and the Union of Soviet Socialist Republics (USSR) was in the process of being created. The Irish question, which had dominated national politics for years, was particularly divisive throughout Great Britain and the revolution in Russia was a beacon to socialists everywhere. At the same time it greatly unsettled the establishment, who feared what they perceived as the 'Bolshevik menace'.

Conrad Noel made his mark on Thaxted as soon as he arrived. He immediately ended the practice whereby seats in church were reserved for wealthy parishioners, which discriminated against the poor. Previously, if the service was crowded, poor people would be excluded altogether. However it was Noel's Irish and socialist sympathies that proved most controversial.

Shortly after the 1916 Easter Rising in Dublin, he was given a Sinn Féin (Irish nationalist) flag by one of his parishioners, an Irish lady. This he set beside the English St George's flag in the church. Soon after that he added a red flag, the emblem of socialism. He also set up a chapel in honour of John Ball, the priest and martyr prominent in the Peasant Revolt of 1381. These actions went largely unnoticed until Noel moved the flags to a more prominent position early in 1921. At that time the Irish insurrection had become very bloody. A visiting Cambridge student enquired why there was wasn't a Union flag in the church and Conrad Noel responded by stating that, in his opinion, the Union flag was imperialist and oppressive. This it would seem was the trigger for the *Battle of the Flags*.

On 21st April 1921 hundreds of students arrived from Cambridge. They forced their way into the church and tore down the offending flags. Undeterred, Noel put the flags back up despite numerous threats. Meanwhile in parliament a member enquired of the Home Secretary, 'What steps are being taken in regard to the preaching of sedition in Thaxted Church?'

On 'Empire Day', May 24th, thousands of demonstrators poured into Thaxted and held a rowdy meeting at the Guildhall. However, Noel had help from what were described as the 'Lansbury Lambs', a group of hefty ex-police officers*. The 'Lambs' infiltrated the demonstrators and discovered some of them had brought a large lorry full of stones. The lorry was commandeered and driven away. It was emptied and had its tyres cut in an attempt to prevent some of the demonstrators from stoning the vicarage as well as all houses not flying a Union flag.

Following the Empire Day troubles the 'Red Vicar', as he had become known, arranged the offending flags hung high up in the Chancel out of reach. This proved no deterrent to his opponents. On the 9th July the church was stormed again. This time the intruders, carrying ladders, forced their way past the police. The two flags were ripped down despite the best efforts of the vicar, who even chased one of the protesters up a ladder. The confiscated flags were then taken to the Bull Ring, just outside the church, where the red flag was ceremoniously burnt – although another was soon acquired.

Two days later, on 11th July, both sides in Ireland agreed a truce and partition came into effect. Northern Ireland was created. This did little to calm the situation in Thaxted.

On and off, for the next 12 months, the *Battle of the Flags* disturbed the peace, with the authorities seemingly powerless to act. Conrad Noel enjoyed widespread support from his parishioners and even won an overwhelming victory in the parish elections. However, a minority group of six well to do parishioners, unhappy that their town had become a focus of trouble week after week, petitioned the Church Authorities in Chelmsford. They argued that the flags had been placed in the church 'without faculty' or in contravention of church regulations.

Thaxted Church. The Eye of the Storm

On Saturday 8th July 1922, the Church Consistory Court at Chelmsford convened in the Shire Hall to consider the petition. The presiding judge was the Chancellor of the Chelmsford Diocese. After lengthy argument from both sides the Chancellor ruled the flags, which were brought to court and displayed as 'evidence', were not religious symbols, but ornaments or decoration. As such they were illegal under ecclesiastical law.

Conrad Noel accepted the judgement and the *Battle of the Flags* was over. This did not stop him running up the red flag at the Church during the general strike of 1926 or hoisting it every May Day for years to come. The 'Red Vicar' stayed in post until he died in 1942.

Conrad's successor was another radical priest, Jack Putterill, the former curate in Thaxted, who was married to Barbara, Conrad Noel's daughter.

After all the trouble it had caused, by the time of Noel's death the Red Flag was honoured nationally as the Soviet Union had become our ally in the desperate fight against Nazi Germany. The flamboyant Countess of Warwick, who was instrumental in bringing Conrad Noel to Thaxted, fought her own battles too. She wholeheartedly embraced Fabian Socialism and seemed to have the ambition to create a hothouse of socialist thought and ideas through her regular salons at Easton Lodge. Amongst her many visitors there were Ramsay MacDonald, the firebrand socialist and trades-unionist, Manny Shinwell, H.G.Wells and George Bernard Shaw.

Daisy Greville was also a leading socialite who notoriously became embroiled in several affairs with prominent men, most famously Albert Edward, The Prince of Wales, who was later King Edward VII. In her role as royal mistress she became the subject of endless society gossip and later when the affair ended, she attempted to blackmail the royal family by publishing intimate letters written to her by the future king.

* *These 'Lambs' had been dismissed from the police for going on strike. They were nicknamed Lansbury's Lambs after the socialist mayor of Poplar George Lansbury.*

THE SECOND WORLD WAR

Despite the effects of the general strike and political tensions in the country at large, the period between the 'Battle of the Flags' and WW2 was relatively peaceful in Essex. With fears rising over Germany's rearmament and ambitions to rule Europe gathering pace, the royal family decided it was prudent to change their family name of 'Saxe-Coburg' to that of 'Windsor'. After the death of King George V, his son Edward VIII, who was known to have German sympathies, decided to abdicate and his brother George VI was crowned. Earlier antipathy to Germany had prompted Britain to rename the 'German Ocean' as the 'North Sea'.

The LCC were pressing ahead with slum clearance plans in London's east end and the building of the huge Becontree Estate. At the same time Henry Ford decided to make Dagenham the centre of his car production in England. His factory would contribute to the prosperity of south Essex by eventually employing up to 50,000 people, many of whom would be housed in the Becontree Estate. A little further east, at East Tilbury, Thomas Bata brought to the area from Czechoslovakia a revolutionary way of working. He built his Bata shoe factory and with it a small town with everything his employees needed supplied by the company. Through its philosophy of, 'A happy worker is a good worker,' the company became the major employer in the area.

Further north, near Braintree, Francis Crittall adopted the same philosophy. In 1925, near the tiny hamlet of Silver End, he built a self-sufficient village for a population of seven to eight thousand people. Crittall wanted his workers to be content and to this end supplied them with every modern convenience. The company thrived and became the biggest manufacturer of steel windows in the world as well as a major Essex employer.

Yet war clouds were gathering and on Sunday 3rd September 1939 the Prime Minister, Neville Chamberlain, broadcast to the nation that a state of war existed between Britain and Germany following the German refusal to withdraw their troops from Poland. Later the same day the first 'wartime' death in Essex was reported when Mrs Emily Bone, a 77 year old widow from Upminster, collapsed and died following the shock of hearing an air raid siren being tested nearby.

Unlike during the First World War, there was a real fear of invasion and the threat of attack from the air led to plans to evacuate vulnerable people from target areas being put into immediate effect.

EVACUATION

London, and particularly the industrial areas, were considered a prime target for enemy bombs and the first priority of civil defence planning was to evacuate children. Evacuation had been an integral part of civil defence planning, despite the Prime Minister's 1938 assurances of 'Peace in Our Time'. Accordingly, London's East End and the West Essex boroughs such as Barking, West Ham and Walthamstow already had well-rehearsed evacuation plans in place. However, following sustained local protests Dagenham and most of Ilford, originally classed as 'neutral' zones, were also included in the evacuation planning.

For the people of Dagenham and Ilford, preparing children for evacuation with no rehearsal was very confusing. Schools were closed but the evacuation plans required a lengthy and complex registration process, made worse by the lack of information coming from the authorities. Official lists stated what an evacuee should take with them; a gas mask and a suitcase with spare clothing, a towel, soap, toothbrush, comb, waterproof boots and food for the trip. This posed problems as many families had only one suitcase, if any, between them and very little in the way of spare clothing. Even if all the requirements could be met, smaller children were unable to lift the packed suitcase! Every child also required an identity card. The children and their parents had no idea where they were going or how they were getting there. The destination was the 'country' but nowhere specific was mentioned.

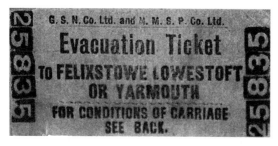

Evacuation ticket by ship issued by Dagenham Borough Council

One favoured evacuation route was by ship from Dagenham Dock. Pleasure steamers, such as the *Medway Queen* and *Royal Sovereign*, would take the evacuees to Yarmouth, Lowestoft or Felixstowe. On the day designated for evacuation, children were to meet at their school with their suitcase, collect an identity card and shipping ticket (or evacuation ticket, see previous page), then take a bus to Ford's jetty at Dagenham Dock. It was decreed that embarkation had to take place early in the morning, before the working day began, so as not to interfere with Ford's war production. However the plans kept changing. In one instance children, escorted by their parents, arrived at the docks in the pouring rain only to be sent back to re-register. To add to the confusion, once evacuation began, the Ministry decided that the total number of evacuees should not exceed 20,000 due to accommodation shortages.

Throughout September and October 1939 there was no bombing. The great calamity everyone expected hadn't happened. Many evacuees returned home, preferring to face the danger from the Luftwaffe than endure the poor food and accommodation at their destinations. It was the time of the so called 'Phoney War'.

On the east coast, Clacton-on-Sea was initially declared a safe haven when war was declared. The town became home to many evacuees from London. The 'Phoney War' ended in 1940. In February a floating mine badly damaged Clacton's pier and on 20th April an enemy plane crashed on 25 Victoria Road, killing the occupants Mr and Mrs Frederick Gill; the first civilian war deaths in England. Suddenly Clacton was in the front line and most of the residents were evacuated along with new arrivals from London. The population of Clacton shrank from 25,000 to just below 5,000 and special permits were needed to even visit the town.

DEFENDING THE ESTUARY

For the first few months of the war Essex saw little or no air activity and no land action. The war at sea was a different matter. Enemy surface raiders and U-boats actively targeted British shipping from day one of the conflict. From October 1939, the Luftwaffe were also dropping mines in the Thames estuary and along the approaches to Harwich. By year end more than two dozen merchant ships and warships had been sunk, including *HMS Gipsy*, a G-class destroyer which had hit a mine in Harwich harbour killing 30 of her crew, including the captain. The defence of the Thames approaches and Harwich port rapidly became high priority. Seven armed towers (or 'Maunsell Forts', named after their designer Guy Maunsell), were built across the Thames approaches, under the code name 'UNCLE'. Their function was to report on approaching enemy air raids, deter German aircraft from using the Thames as a landmark and to prevent attempts at aerial mine laying in these important shipping channels. A boom was also built, stretching from Shoeburyness in Essex to Sheerness in Kent, to prevent enemy vessels sneaking up river.

Rough Towers 1942 – a navy fort. They were also known colloquially as 'Uncles'

Of the seven forts, four of them - Rough Towers, Sunk Head, Tongue Sands and Knock John, were crewed by the Royal Navy. These four each comprised two cylindrical towers built onto a sunken concrete barge securely pinned to the seabed. The towers were topped by a gun platform, where two 3.75-inch guns and two 40 mm Bofors guns were mounted. The forts, weighing some 4,500 tons, were built and fitted out in Northfleet in Kent, then towed out to sea to be sunk in position with the crew already on board.*

The three remaining forts, Nore, Red Sands and Shivering Sands were manned by the army. They were designed for anti-aircraft defence and were larger installations than the navy forts, comprising seven towers supporting interconnected steel platforms (see page 145). Four of the towers carried QF 3.75 inch anti-aircraft guns, arranged in a semicircle ahead of the control centre and crew accommodation. On the towers to the rear of the control centre, 40mm Bofors guns were mounted. The seventh tower, set to one side of the gun towers and further out, was the searchlight tower.

All the forts were decommissioned in the late 1950s. Of the navy forts, Rough Towers, some 7.5 miles off Harwich, was acquired by the Bates family in 1967 who later named it, *The Principality of Sealand,* the smallest independent country in international waters - a claim unrecognised by any international authority. Sunk Head Fort was destroyed by the Royal Engineers in August 1967, leaving nothing above the waterline. Tongue Fort stood until 1996 when it collapsed in a storm. Knock John Fort was for a short time the base of the 'pirate' *Essex Radio.* It survives today though in a somewhat dilapidated state.

Of the Army forts, The Nore, midway between Sheerness and Shoebury, was badly damaged in 1953 when the Norwegian ship *Baalbek* collided with it, destroying two of the towers and killing four civilians. The ruins were dismantled in 1959/60. Red Sands fort, consisting of seven towers at the mouth of the Thames Estuary, had all its linking walk ways and scaling ladders removed to prevent unauthorised occupation. A little further out, 9.2 miles from land, due north of Herne Bay, is the Shivering Sands group made-up of several towers which was once home to *Radio Sutch* (see also the Battle of the Airwaves page 143).

* *Only Rough Towers Fort was sunk in position with the crew aboard. After a near capsizing during its positioning the plan was abandoned. The admiralty ordered crews to remain on the support barge until the subsequent forts were fully secured to the seabed.*

THE LITTLE SHIPS OF LEIGH

On the 10th May 1940 the Prime Minister, Neville Chamberlain, resigned and was replaced by Winston Churchill, who promptly formed a wartime coalition government. On the same day the German Army invaded France, Belgium and Holland, sweeping aside all opposition. The British Expeditionary Force (BEF), along with elements of French forces, was forced to retreat before this onslaught. A German spearhead reached the sea, leaving the allied forces trapped in a small area of coast around Dunkirk.

On the 26th May a contingency plan to evacuate the troops, code named *Operation Dynamo*, was put into action by the admiralty. From the commander on Southend Pier, already requisitioned by the Navy as *HMS Leigh,* requests were made for volunteer crews and their shallow draft vessels to help in the rescue mission.

The response from the Essex fishermen of Leigh was immediate. Arthur Dench was the first to report with his boat *Letitia.* He was quickly joined by five other Leigh cockle boats, the *Defender, Endeavour, Reliance, Renown* and *Resolute*, and their crews. These six boats, under the overall control of Sub-Lieutenant Solomon RN, left Southend Pier at 11:00am on the 31st May bound for Dunkirk.

The restored Endeavour at Leigh-on-Sea

Although coming under attack from German bombers, they arrived at close to seven in the evening and promptly set about ferrying stranded troops from the beach to the larger ships anchored in deeper waters.

These Leigh Bawleys, with their broad beam and flattish bottoms, designed to cope with the Thames estuary sandbanks, were ideally suited for this work. The ships, averaging only thirty feet long and ten feet wide, between them rescued many thousands of soldiers. The total rescued by the armada of small boats commandeered for this operation was in excess of three hundred thousand. In the early hours of June 1st the Leigh men started for home. The *Renown* had developed engine trouble and at 1:15 am her crew hailed the *Letitia* who took her in tow. Thirty-five minutes later, as Arthur Dench recalled, 'A terrible explosion took place, the *Renown* hit a mine and a hail of wood splinters came down on our deck. In the pitch dark we could do nothing except pull in the tow-rope, which was just as we had passed it out to the *Renown* three-quarters of an hour before, But not a sign of the *Renown*'.

The rest of the Leigh boats continued to Ramsgate then on to Leigh-on-Sea where they were met by their families, who were waiting at the waterside. Arthur Dench said of the *Renown's* crew, 'They knew nothing of war. They went to save, not to fight.....It was a small tragedy in the great disaster of those days of war yet great in the hearts of Leigh people'.

In May 1968 these events were commemorated at St Clements Church by a plaque and flags being dedicated in the Chapel of the Resurrection. In 1972, in the churchyard, a memorial was erected to the fishermen of Leigh, and specifically Frank and Leslie Osborne, Harry Noakes and Harold Graham Porter, the crew of the *Renown*. The *Endeavour* is the only surviving Leigh boat of those that went to Dunkirk. Registered with the 'Association of Dunkirk Little Ships', it has now been extensively restored.

On the 13th May 1940, Churchill, in his first address to the House of Commons, said, 'I would say to the House as I said to those who have joined this government: I have nothing to offer but blood, toil, tears and sweat. We have before us an ordeal of the most grievous kind. We have before us many, many long months of struggle and of suffering'. And yet on 1st June 1940, the weekly newspaper *Essex Newsman* cheerfully reported that the British Expeditionary Force was coming home after 'gallant fighting in Flanders'. It said all the men were in splendid heart and reported terrific German losses in their drive to the Channel ports. This contrasts with the Prime Minister's words, just three days later, on 4th June, when, whilst acknowledging what had been achieved in rescuing 338,000 allied troops as 'a miracle of deliverance', he added, 'Wars are not won by evacuations'. He also said there was no doubt in his mind that the last few weeks had been a 'colossal military disaster', with the BEF having had to abandon all its heavy armour and equipment. The 2nd battalion of the Essex Regiment was deployed to France in September 1939. In May 1940 the battalion took part in the retreat and withdrawal from Dunkirk, managing to return virtually unscathed.

CONCRETE, WIRE AND MINEFIELDS

With the German Army on the verge of complete victory in France and Belgium it seemed inevitable that an invasion of Great Britain would shortly follow. Churchill spoke to the nation to record perhaps his most memorable lines. 'We shall defend our island, whatever the cost may be. We shall fight on the beaches, we shall fight on the landing grounds, we shall fight in the fields and in the streets, we shall fight in the hills; we shall never surrender.'

With the British Army weakened by having abandoned much of its equipment in France, urgent plans were put in hand to build a series of static defensive lines around Britain. The first line of defence was on the coast where hundreds of pillboxes, many to a design, unique to the county, called the 'The Essex Lozenge', were built. These concrete pillboxes were octagonal shaped and elongated so as to sit atop and astride the sea wall. They had three firing windows, at the front and rear, and two at each end of the long side walls. This design allowed fire in all directions in the event of enemy attack. More than thirty of these lozenges still exist along the coast.

One of the more unusual features were the so called anti-tank pimples installed at strategic points on roads running inland from the coast. These cone shape structures (see page 104/105), made of concrete, approximately three feet high were designed to impede the movement of enemy tanks. Although most were installed in coastal towns such as Clacton or Southend, several were put up in Colchester and Chelmsford. One set that has been preserved by the Heritage Conservation branch of

Essex County Council is at Winchester Court on the Broomfield Road just north of Chelmsford.

An even more robust barrier to tanks was provided by long lines of anti-tank cubes, shown at the bottom of page 105. Made of reinforced concrete, over 1800 cubes were cast in situ along the coast in rows sometimes two or three deep. Two surviving cubes have been built into the seawall 500 yards east of the Kursaal in Southend-on-Sea.

At the same time access to the beaches was denied to all except authorised personnel. In turn the beaches were covered with entanglements of barbed wire and beach scaffolding to prevent enemy troops or vehicles coming ashore. Minefields were also laid on both Shoeburyness and Clacton seafronts. The piers at Walton-on-the-Naze and Clacton, considered ideal for the potential landing of enemy troops, were partially dismantled. Clacton's other pier, on west beach, the 'Jetty Amusement Centre', originally a landing stage, was completely demolished. The war was an economic disaster for seaside resorts.

Inland over 50 defensive lines were constructed around the nation. Protecting London from the east was the Eastern Command line that ran along the River Colne, past Colchester and then into Suffolk.
Nearer to the capital was the GHQ (or General Headquarters) Line. In Essex it ran northwards from Canvey Island to Great Chesterford just north of Saffron Walden. It roughly followed the route of the present day A130 to Great Dunmow. Nearly 400 pill boxes were built along this section, of which over 100 still survive.

It seemed that pillboxes were built everywhere in all shapes and sizes - hexagonal, mushroom and even retractable ones embedded in airport runways. Pillboxes surrounded strategic points. In a radius of just three miles, 50 were put up in Rochford alone, guarding the airport. Another cluster in Canewdon, just south of the River Crouch, protected a major radar development site. Whilst the radar station is long gone numerous pillboxes remain and seem immovable despite the passage of over 70 years.

DEFENCE LINES ACROSS ESSEX

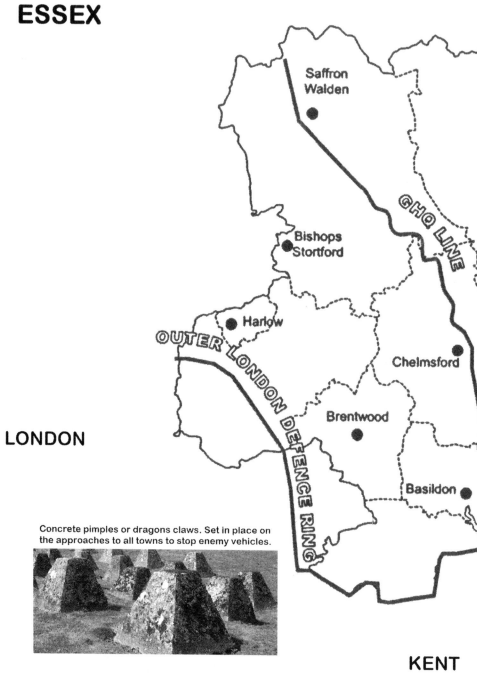

Saffron
Walden

GHQ LINE

Bishops
Stortford

Harlow

OUTER LONDON DEFENCE RING

Chelmsford

LONDON

Brentwood

Basildon

Concrete pimples or dragons claws. Set in place on
the approaches to all towns to stop enemy vehicles.

KENT

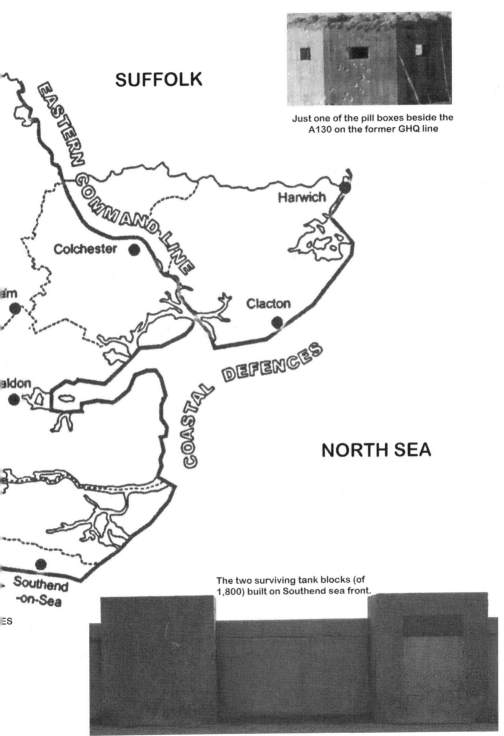

SUFFOLK

Just one of the pill boxes beside the
A130 on the former GHQ line

Harwich

Colchester

Clacton

aldon

NORTH SEA

Southend
-on-Sea

The two surviving tank blocks (of
1,800) built on Southend sea front.

HMS LEIGH AND HMS WESTCLIFF

Southend, for many years, has been known for having the longest pier in the world. The original, 1830 wooden pier at only 600 feet long was unusable at low tide and was extended in 1846 to 7,000 feet making it the longest in Europe. Sixty years later the wooden pier was replaced by a new iron structure complete with an electric railway designed by James Brunlees. By 1929 a 'New Pier Head', complete with upper deck, plus the Prince George Extension, brought the pier's length up to 1.34 miles; the longest pleasure pier in the world. Though famous as a tourist attraction, during World War II it was to play a prominent part in naval defences of the Thames estuary and particularly in the rescue of troops from Dunkirk (see page 100).

Nine days after the outbreak of war, Southend Pier, already closed to the public, was requisitioned by the navy. Renamed *HMS Leigh* it stayed under navy control for the duration of the war. In the event of an invasion, a military standing order was put in place for the senior officer on duty to blow it up. From a control room on the pier head the Navy could organise shipping movements in the Thames estuary. During the five years of conflict the pier served as a mustering point for 3,367 convoys, comprising 84,297 vessels.

By 1942 Southend, like Clacton, was a closed town, out of bounds to all except the military and those residents who had not been compulsorily relocated for the duration of the war. The whole area as far west as Chalkwell was renamed *HMS Westcliff*. It became a training base and naval transit camp containing at times more than 3,000 military personnel. Training of formed flotillas was carried out and it was also a holding base for Royal Marines' landing craft and Combined Operations personnel. In 1943 Lord Mountbatten visited *HMS Westcliff*. As head of Combined Operations, the unit responsible for developing the skills of seaborne landings, he emphasised the importance of this area in the training for the assault on the beaches of Normandy.

Both *HMS Leigh* and *HMS Westcliff* were decommissioned in 1946. The beaches and the pier were gradually returned to civilian use and by 1949 the pier had reached its peak of popularity with seven million visitors recorded.

Southend Pier (formerly HMS Leigh)

AIR DEENCES

Following the same pattern as the GHQ lines to protect London against land attack (see page 104/105), a ring of air defences were put in place. Closest to the coast were observers. London was then encircled by an outer gun zone that in Essex more or less followed the GHQ line. Between that and London was what was described as the aircraft fighting area.

In the front line. Defending the capital

These defences, supplemented by the Thames estuary forts and anti-aircraft bases along the River Thames, were designed to make life difficult for enemy aircraft using the Thames as their guide to bombing London. For example, at Foulness aircraft would be met by the 3.7 inch guns at Fisherman's Head, Ridgemarsh Farm and New Burwood. After Foulness, the guns at Great Wakering and Sutton would take over.

Seconds later, these would be joined by the batteries of Hawkwell, Rayleigh and Sandpit Hill at Hadleigh. Of the World War II heavy anti-aircraft gun sites only that one at Sutton, just north of Southend, and now a Scheduled Monument, remains.

After the Outer Gun Zone came the Aircraft Fighting Area. Here the airfields were rapidly upgraded. Hainault Farm, originally an airstrip in the First World War, was located about half a mile from Fairlop. In 1940 a new airfield was constructed using many of the Hainault Farm buildings. It became known as RAF Fairlop. The airfield became operational in September 1941 with the arrival of No. 603 Squadron, flying spitfires, previously stationed at Hornchurch. Nearby Hainault Lodge, demolished in 1973 and now a nature reserve, was used as accommodation for some of the officers. The station was also home to No. 24 Balloon Centre with four squadrons forming part of the balloon barrage around London. The Balloon Centre was disbanded in February 1945 and the airfield closed in August 1946. Later the site was cleared and, after some years of gravel extraction, was developed as a country park with a boating lake and a golf course, now known as Fairlop Waters.

In 1939 Southend Municipal Airport was requisitioned by the Air Ministry and designated RAF Rochford as a satellite airfield. During WW2 it was a base for fighter squadrons. After the war Rochford reverted to being a municipal airport and was the third busiest airport in Britain during the 1960s-70s. Southend Council sold the airport to the Stobart Group in 2008 since when, after many improvements, it has become 'London Southend Airport'.

The WW1 Royal Air Force Station Hornchurch was upgraded in 1928 to be the home of a fighter station able to face future defence needs. Close to the Thames and just 14 miles from central London, it was ideally placed to be, together with RAF Rochford, a sector airfield of RAF Fighter Command 11 Group. Covering London and the south east, together they played a crucial role in the 1940 Battle of Britain. Hornchurch went on to become the Aircrew Selection Centre for many years until 'Flying Training Command' moved to RAF Biggin Hill. The station closed in July 1962 and today very little of the site remains. It is now covered by Hornchurch Country Park and housing.

Debden, three miles southeast of Saffron Walden, was the Sector Station of No.11 Group RAF during the Battle of Britain. Commissioned in 1937, its hard surface runways were only laid in 1940, yet during August and September of that year, Debden fighters claimed seventy aircraft destroyed, thirty probables and forty-one damaged. On 28th January 1941, the station was visited by King George VI and Queen Elizabeth, and seven days later by a German aircrew! On 4th February 1941 a German pilot landed his aircraft and taxied to the control tower, then realising his mistake rapidly took off again.

Up to September 1942 Debden was home to various Squadrons flying Spitfires. After that date the airfield was transferred to the United States Eighth Air Force and was assigned 'USAAF designation Station 356'. The American fighters were active in the invasion of Normandy in June 1944, the airborne invasion of the Netherlands in September and the airborne assault across the Rhine in March 1945. After the ceasefire they left Debden to return to the USA. The airfield later became home to the RAF police training school until it finally closed in August 1975.

A 'Hawker Hurricane' originally based at RAF North Weald

North Weald Airfield, which played a prominent role in WW1, was also strategically important in WW2. From there RAF Hawker Hurricanes and Bristol Blenheim night fighters saw action over the beaches of Dunkirk and in the Battle of Britain. Later, American 'Eagle' Squadrons, flying Spitfires, were based there and in 1942 two Norwegian squadrons of Spitfires moved there. After the war, in 1949, Gloster Meteors and de Havilland Vampire jet fighters had arrived at North Weald and the last RAF combat unit, '111 Squadron', which contained the famous Black Arrows formation team, left in 1958. The RAF severed connection with the airfield in 1964 and it was sold in 1979 to Epping Forest District Council. It operates today as a busy civil airfield.

A partially exposed Anderson shelter. Over 3.5 million were built

One of the results of air raids was a boom in the construction of 'Anderson' air raid shelters. Designed in 1938 and named after Sir John Anderson, the Minister of Home Security, they were relatively simple to construct and could hold six people.

The main part of the shelter was formed from six corrugated steel panels curved at one end. Once assembled the shelters were buried four feet deep in the ground then covered over with a thick layer of soil and turf.

They were quite cramped and someone taller than 6ft would not have been able to stand. Approximately 3.5 million Anderson shelters were built either before the war had started or during the conflict and for those on a low income they were supplied free, otherwise the cost was £7.00. During the Second Word War aircraft bombing was much more severe than during WWI. The Essex Police recorded over 150,000 bombs of various types being dropped on the county between 1939 and 1945. A further 511 V1 Rockets and 400 V2 rockets landed in Essex, although many of the former were shot down. Additionally 530 parachute mines were dropped in the waters around the Essex coastline. 850 people were listed as killed in the county, including the Mayor of Chelmsford, John Ockleford Thompson, his wife Emma and his son Thomas, when a bomb fell on their house in London Road, Chelmsford.

A month after the catastrophe at Dunkirk and with all of Western Europe under Nazi domination, Hitler turned his attention to invading the British Isles. In order to achieve this it was essential for the Luftwaffe to gain air superiority. In July 1940 the 'Battle of Britain' began. To begin with, enemy attacks were concentrated on coastal targets and allied shipping in the English Channel. The main offensive followed in August where it was hoped to destroy RAF Fighter Command. Airfields, especially those in the south-east, were targeted. On 30th/31st August, Germany launched over 1,310 sorties against Britain. In Essex, RAF stations at Rochford, Hornchurch, Debden and North Weald were struck by waves of fighter aircraft and bombers. The Luftwaffe, however, had overestimated the damage it had inflicted and wrongly concluded that the RAF was a spent force. On 7th September, the Germans shifted the weight of their attacks away from RAF targets to London; a move which gave British airfields time to recover and go back on the attack. With the Luftwaffe suffering unsustainable losses, their air superiority was further away than ever. In September, Hitler postponed operation 'Sea Lion', the code name for the invasion of Britain, indefinitely. It was also during the height of the Battle of Britain that, on 20th August 1940, Winston Churchill made another of his defining speeches to the House of Commons, which included his tribute to the fighter pilots, 'Never in the history of mankind have so many owed so much to so few'.

STATION 43

With the Second World War in full flow the Government, using powers that been on the statute book since a Defence Act of 1842, requisitioned many stately houses in England for training or command and control purposes. One such house was Audley End near Saffron Walden. Saffron Walden straddled what was called the General Headquarters line (page 104/105). Still evident around the town today are decommissioned bridge barriers, pillboxes and anti-tank blocks.

Audley End House is one of England's finest country houses, built in the 16th century on the site of a former Benedictine Abbey, by Sir Thomas Audley. Since then its owners have included King Charles II and generations of Earls of Suffolk. Finally it became the family seat of Sir John Griffin Griffin, the first Baron Braybrooke. The house was offered to the government by the 7th baron's family and requisitioned in March 1941. Initially it became a base for the home guard and a headquarters for co-ordinating local defence efforts. Many of the rooms were fitted with wooden screens to protect the interior of the house from damage and some of the gardens were dug up to grow vegetables.

By the spring of 1942, the threat of land invasion had receded and Audley End was given a new purpose. Though there had been speculation over the future of the house, none of it had included the Special Operations Executive (SOE, the forerunner of MI6) taking charge. By May 1942 Audley End was designated 'Special Training School 43', known as Station 43. The SOE was operating underground warfare courses and was the official headquarters of the Polish section. A tight veil of secrecy was drawn over the whole establishment and virtually all contact between locals and the occupants of the house was prohibited. The estate became a training school for agents to be sent on dangerous missions to occupied Europe. In Winston Churchill's words, both men and women would learn the arts of 'ungentlemanly warfare'.

Although Poland had been overrun by the Nazis in September 1939, then later divided between Hitler's forces and those of the Soviet Union, large numbers of the Polish military escaped to Great Britain. It was from these that trainees at Audley End were drawn. Selection was tough both physically and psychologically and only a small percentage of those who applied were accepted. Between 1942 and 1944 over 500 recruits graduated.

Whilst the local residents of Saffron Walden had little idea of what was going on at the 'big house' and perhaps considered it prudent not to ask questions, there was plenty of unofficial contact with the trainees. During the courses, apart from learning about weapons handling, explosives and communications, trainees undertook specialist driving courses and how to best disseminate black propaganda. Small groups of men were sent on missions into rural Essex. In one case a group was sent to rob a post office. Mock sabotage attempts were made on stations, rolling stock and bridges. Fake attacks were made on army check points and airfields. Burglaries were a feature, where trainees were despatched into the countryside to hone their breaking and entering skills and practice microfilm photography. Of course in all of the incidents outlined above any property taken was returned and damage repaired. Yet nothing was ever reported to the public as all the operations were cloaked in the official secrets act.

One of the most challenging tasks facing a recruit was to be driven miles away from their base in the dead of night and dropped off without maps or supplies and told to make their way back covertly to Audley End. Should a trainee be caught (picked up by the Home Guard or police), they would be deemed to have failed the course and be unsuitable. What is perhaps amazing is that during all these clandestine nocturnal activities which took place when strict wartime blackout restrictions were in force, only two deaths were notified. However, it is not clear from the surviving records whether these deaths were amongst the Polish trainees, the British military or police or even civilians.

On completion of training, agents were sent in the main to Poland to coordinate with local resistance and to feed back intelligence. It was extremely dangerous work. The Polish War Memorial at Audley End records the deaths of 108 Polish agents serving with SOE. Several agents were killed before arriving at their target through their planes being brought down or problems with their parachutes. However, once on the ground, an impressive list of several thousand acts of sabotage were recorded. These included 92,000 faults built into enemy artillery shells.

Such was the success of the SOE graduates that they became known as 'Cichociemni' which translates as 'The Silent Unseen'.

Station 43 remained operational until December 1944. The Polish training section was then transferred to newly liberated Italy which offered a shorter flying time to Poland. The army relinquished control of Audley End with the conclusion of the Second World War.

The Braybrooke family moved back in briefly but found the cost of restoring and maintaining such a large house impossible. In 1948 the Ministry of Works bought the house and grounds for the nation and since 1984 the property has been cared for by English Heritage.

Left. The Polish War Memorial at Audley End

****

The course of World War II changed dramatically in 1941. Hitler turned his attention away from a land invasion of the British Isles and focused on the USSR. On 22ⁿᵈ June massed formations of German troops supported by tanks, heavy artillery and aircraft struck eastwards in Operation Barbarossa whose aim was to destroy the Soviet Union. Five months later, on the other side of the world, on the morning of December 7th, carrier borne aircraft from the Japanese Imperial Navy launched a surprise attack on the US Pacific naval base at Pearl Harbor in Hawaii. The attack led to the United States' entry into World War II. Four days after the Japanese attack on Pearl Harbor, Nazi Germany declared war on the USA. The British Empire, which had fought alone against the might of Nazi Germany, now had two potential powerful allies.

Although the Battle of Britain had ended with the RAF gaining the upper hand, German bombers were still active over the British mainland. The targets were population centres and industry and night time bombing was very heavy in the first six months of 1941. On May 10th the Luftwaffe launched an unprecedented assault on London, later described as the worst night of the blitz. At 11pm, air raid sirens sounded. By the following morning, bombs had claimed 1,486 lives, destroyed 11,000 homes and hit the Houses of Parliament, Waterloo Station, the British Museum and many other landmark buildings. The previous day seventeen workers had been killed in an airstrike at the Marconi factory in Chelmsford. Both Marconi and the Hoffmann Ball Bearing factory were crucial to the war effort and therefore targets for German bombs. Though Essex at large was not always a deliberate target, enemy aircraft often randomly ditched unspent ordinance on the county as they returned to their bases. Numerous German aircraft also crashed in Essex after being damaged by ground fire or RAF fighters.

THE AMERICANS ARE COMING
LAUNCH PAD

For almost as long as many people can remember, the UK Government has been agonising over where to build an additional airport runway in the south-east. Gatwick, Stansted and Heathrow, as suitable locations, have all been subjected to in depth inquiries and public consultations costing many millions of pounds. The Thames Estuary sites of Maplin Sands, just off the Essex coast, and Cliffe in Kent have also been considered, again at great expense. Both were rejected. However, in October 2016 the Government indicated that Heathrow was its preferred choice although it would allow at least another year of consultation before a final decision was made.

Yet history shows that there is nothing like a war to concentrate the collective mind and get things done. After the US entry into the Second World War, air bases in Britain became a priority. Within just 20 months, fifteen airfields in Essex alone, each with a runway at least as long as present day 'London Southend Airport' were conceived, constructed and became operational. They were to be home for hundreds of American fighter bombers and support aircraft. With them came more than 200,000 military and civilian personnel of the United States 9th Air Force, who were billeted in the Essex countryside. The new airfields were primarily used as launching points for tactical air support operations as opposed to serving as bases for heavy bombers.

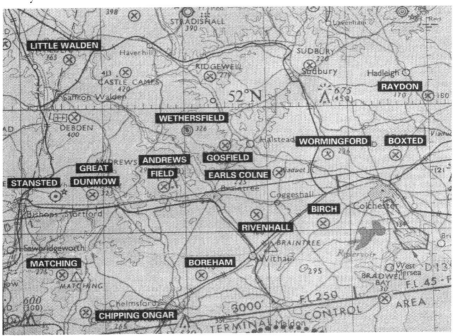

US bases built in Essex in the space of 20 months.
Raydon is just across the county border in Suffolk

As preparations for the allied invasion of continental Europe began to take shape, the American force grew in size with fighter bomber, troop carrier, air defence, engineering and service commands. Their objectives were to support allied invading forces on the ground, neutralise opposing forces, attack communications, destroy ammunition dumps and harass the enemy's retreat, as well as provide reconnaissance. Although the aircraft and most of the personnel didn't arrive in England until late 1943, US army engineers and private contractors had been busy for a year, building or refurbishing airfields in Essex in anticipation of their arrival.

In June 1943, the first Essex airfield to become operational for the 9th Air Force, with a complement of Martin B-26 Marauder bombers, was Great Saling (Station 485) to the west of Braintree. It was also called Andrews Field in honour of the commanding general Frank Andrews who was killed when his aircraft crashed earlier in the war. Great Saling was also the first to be constructed by US army engineers. A little further to the south west, Willingale (or Chipping Ongar), Station 162, became operational a month later. Rubble resulting from the blitz in London was used as hard core for the runways, which in turn, after the war, was used as foundations for the Brentwood bypass section of the A12.

The 'B26', the backbone of the 9th Airforce

By December 1943, missions were being undertaken from the airfields of Earls Colne, Great Dunmow, Gosfield, Boxted and Wormingford.

With the build up to 'D' Day in June 1944, the 9th US Air Force was at full strength despatching daily an average of 1,000 aircraft to strike enemy targets. Following the 'D' Day invasion and the rapid progress of the allied forces inland, coupled with advances in Italy, Essex began to lose its strategic importance as a launch pad for tactical air support. By December nearly all the units of the 9th US Air Force had been redeployed to bases in liberated France or Italy.

Today nearly all of the former US air fields in Essex have been closed. Many have been broken up and returned to farmland or developed for industry. There are exceptions. Stansted Mountfichet (Station 169) is now Stansted Airport although there is almost no trace of any of the original wartime features. Wethersfield (Station 170), near the village of Finchingfield, is now used by the Ministry of Defence police and also by civil police as a training centre, although there are nascent plans to develop the site for housing. Boreham (Station No 161), to the east of Chelmsford, once a motor racing circuit in 1949-52, is now home to the Essex Police Air Support Unit and occasionally the Essex air ambulance.

Earls Colne (Station No 358) to the north of Colchester served as the headquarters to the US 9th Air Force during its relatively short stay in Essex. A permanent memorial site dedicated to those who served at Earls Colne airfield may be seen at the northern end of the arboretum in the Mark's Hall estate. There are memorials giving information on aircrew casualties and aircraft losses at most of the former Essex airfields still existing.

The year 1942 was relatively quiet as far as Essex was concerned, although industry in Chelmsford was frequently hit. The Hoffman works, established in 1898 in New Street and Rectory Lane, achieved worldwide recognition for precision-made bearings, essential components in military aircraft, vehicles, tank turrets and naval guns. It was said that there were over 1,000 Hoffmann bearings in a Spitfire's Merlin engine and 4,000 in the engines of the Lancaster bomber. So for the enemy, the works were a key target. Four workers were killed and 500 properties nearby were damaged when the factory was bombed in July 1942. In October it was targeted again by a lone plane, flying low, killing another four workers and injuring a further 65. In neighbouring Henry Road, five people died in their homes when a 500 kilogram bomb, deflected off the roof of the assembly shop, exploded at the rear of no 17. Following this attack 30 barrage balloons were raised over Chelmsford to deter future low level air raids.

In the wider war, late 1942 brought some cheer to the allied cause. In Egypt, the British Army, under the command of Bernard Montgomery, won a decisive victory against combined German and Italian forces at El-Alamein. This victory turned the tide of war in North Africa and ended the threat to the Suez Canal, a vital supply line. On the 10th November, in a speech at the Mansion House in London, the Prime Minister Winston Churchill, referring to the success at El-Alamein, included the following lines;

'Now this is not the end. It is not even the beginning of the end. But it is, perhaps, the end of the beginning.'

On the Eastern front, by December, the German Army were cut off and surrounded by Soviet Forces following their failure to capture the city of Stalingrad (now Volgograd) in Southern Russia. After heavy losses the Sixth Army eventually capitulated in February 1943. German forces never regained the initiative in the East.

WAR PRODUCTION

During the conflict it was crucial that the fighting forces on the front line were equipped with not only enough weapons and ammunition to attack the enemy but also the necessary logistical backup to keep them going through thick and thin. This would include everything from food and protective clothing, communications equipment and medical supplies up to trucks and transport. The war effort was in full swing throughout the country and so many Essex companies contributed to it that it is impossible to name all but a few of the major players in the confines of this book.

The Ford Motor Company, on the banks of the Thames at Dagenham, was a key supporter of the war effort. It switched from building cars to producing armoured tracked vehicles as well as engines for all kinds of military trucks. Also, during the war years, 120,000 agricultural tractors, equally essential to speed up farming production, were built. Other figures for industrial production during this period are equally impressive.

Next door to the Ford plant, at the top of Chequers Lane, was Briggs Motor Bodies Ltd. In peacetime this factory produced car bodies and truck cabs for many different vehicle manufacturers. Once the war started, production switched to military vehicle bodies, tanks and even aeroplane parts. Following the fall of Dunkirk, the Ministry of Supply deemed the army's helmets unfit for the type of warfare being experienced. Briggs rose to the challenge and by the war's end had supplied 11 million redesigned helmets. In the same period they also manufactured 20 million jerrycans for fuel as well as 8 million ammunition boxes.

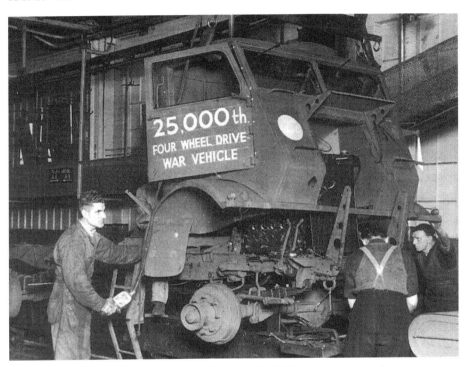

Despite the bombing, production at Ford, Dagenham continued

Adjacent to Briggs, at Dagenham Dock, the Kelsey-Hayes Wheel Company supplied wheels to the motor industry. This company also strove to meet the demands of the military. During the war, in addition to producing over two million wheels of all shapes and sizes for military land vehicles and aircraft as well as tank parts, the company even diversified into manufacturing machine guns. Also at Dagenham Dock, Southern United Telephone Cables Ltd aided military communications, supplying over 25 million miles of telephone line.

Just to the north of Dagenham village the pharmaceutical company, May and Baker Ltd, were heavily engaged in meeting the medical demands of the war. Their famous 'M&B' tablets, the forerunners of today's antibiotics, as well as curing Winston Churchill of pneumonia in 1943, saved many thousands of lives during the fighting. On the other side of Dagenham, in Whalebone Lane, the mattress maker, Springcot Ltd produced 750,000 parachutes and nearly 200,000 sleeping bags.

In the 1950s, Briggs and Kelsey-Hayes were both subsumed into the Ford Empire and their wartime manufacturing facilities are long gone. The Ford works has undergone substantial change since its heyday of the post war years. Whole vehicles are no longer made there, only diesel engines. After the war Springcot Ltd continued to manufacture sisal products such as rope, twine and general cordage until the 1960s when the company closed and the factory was demolished. Southern United Telephone Cables Ltd became Telephone Cables Ltd and went into liquidation in 2013.

In north-east Essex, Woods of Colchester Ltd's factory at Braiswick made industrial fans. As early as 1938 the War Office had contracted Woods to supply fans to be fitted in tank turrets. Fans were in in high demand as they were also needed to cool searchlights and a variety of high performance engines. The war effort could not be undertaken without adequate supplies of paper and stationery. Colchester's E. N. Mason and Sons Arclight Works, of Cowdray Avenue, rose to the challenge. According to company statistics, during the war years they produced 46,000 miles of paper suitable for printing black and white aerial reconnaissance photographs. Additionally 4,500 miles of tracing paper was made which was used to track flying bombs. The company supplied 250,000 bottles of waterproof drawing ink and 650,000 rubber stamps. Another Colchester company making an important contribution to the war effort was Davey Paxman & Company. From two factories at Hythe Hill and the Britannia Works, close to St Botolph's Church, diesel engines were made for warships. Over half of the British Submarines in service were fitted with engines made in Colchester.

In Chelmsford, throughout World War II, the Marconi Company, along with the Southend based Ekco Ltd, continued to develop essential communication equipment for the war effort, including the development and production of the T1154 transmitter and the R1155 receiver. These were used extensively by the Royal Air Force, mainly in larger aircraft such as the Avro Lancaster, Handley Page Halifax, Vickers Wellington and Short Sunderland. Some were used in vehicles and air-sea rescue launches. Both companies were also heavily involved in the development of 'The Chain Home Radar System' which provided the RAF with a 20 minute warning of approaching enemy bombers. The 360 feet high radar towers that stood at Canewdon and Great Bromley were part of a chain of eighty around the country. Research into the technology took place in Great Baddow, which is now home to the complete radar tower which was once stationed at Canewdon; it is the only one of its kind to still be in active service.

As previously mentioned on page 116 Chelmsford was also home to the Hoffmann Manufacturing Company, makers of world class ball bearings. After a series of mergers the Hoffmann Company was wound down and finally closed on 23rd December 1989. The Marconi Company was bought by BAE Systems in 1999; only the New Street buildings, now grade II listed, remain in Chelmsford. Ekco Ltd was taken over by Philips Electronics in 1967, and by 1970, what was once a household name had practically disappeared. The Southend factory site, idle for some years, was cleared for redevelopment in 2008.

All the above companies were regularly bombed during the course of the war, nevertheless most managed to continue in full production.

THE WOODEN WONDER
From Kitchen Cabinets to Bombers

In an effort to maximise aircraft production, the Air Ministry and the aero industry sought the help of the furniture makers of the Lea valley. They requested the furniture industry to convert their production lines from making kitchen cabinets and wardrobes to turning out war machines. A positive response to this seemingly strange request was evident in the manufacture of the 'Mosquito'– or the 'Wooden Wonder' as some called it.

Wood had already been used by aircraft maker de-Havilland for the DH88 Comet, which had won the prestigious 1934 London-Melbourne air race. The Mosquito had been on the drawing board since 1936, in response to the Air Ministry requisition number P.13/36 specifying the manufacture and design of a twin-engine bomber for worldwide use. The design specified a fuselage and wings made entirely of wood. The declaration of war in 1939 gave urgency to its development. In a short time thousands of carpenters were retrained to build wooden aircraft bodies.

The majority of the Mosquitoes were finally assembled in the de-Havilland plants at Hatfield and Leavesden from component parts produced by more than 200 sub-contractors. One of the biggest of these, contracted to build Mosquito fuselages and wings, was the high-class domestic furniture maker, F. Wrighton & Sons Ltd, of Billet Road, Walthamstow. To meet the Air Ministry request, Wrighton & Sons formed a subsidiary company; Wrighton Aircraft Ltd. Furniture making virtually ceased in Walthamstow during the war years and on July 8th 1944, despite regular disruption from bombing, Wrighton produced their 1,000th Mosquito fuselage.

The Mosquito's first operational sortie of the war was on 20th September 1941. It was a reconnaissance mission, photographing harbour facilities in enemy-occupied South West France, flown by Squadron Leader Rupert Clerke. The Mosquito went on to become one of the most versatile aircraft employed in World War II. Over 7,500 were built and apart from being used for photo reconnaissance it was adapted as a night fighter, a fast light bomber and a pathfinder. It ended the war with the lowest loss rate of any aircraft in RAF Bomber Command.

After the war, Wrighton Ltd returned to furniture making. By 1958 the company had achieved a national and international reputation for high quality furniture. At that time the Wrighton Aircraft Ltd subsidiary was being maintained but it finally closed in 1967, the furniture factory closing shortly afterwards. Despite its reputation Wrighton suffered the fate of most of the other quality furniture makers that the Lea Valley was known for; the increasing competition from mass produced and 'flat pack' furniture. Wrighton furniture is today sought after by collectors and there is even a piece of their kitchen furniture in the Victoria & Albert museum.

The Wooden Wonder – made in Walthamstow

Whilst on the subject of wood, the shipyards of the River Colne between Brightlingsea and Wivenhoe were kept extremely busy either building ships or repairing them. In 1942, one yard, the Wivenhoe Shipyard Ltd, started to build minesweepers made entirely of wood. Nearly all were built from oak or elm grown within a twenty five mile radius of Wivenhoe, with each ship using an average of 250 trees in construction. The yard completed 24 minesweepers for the Royal and Dutch Navies during the war.

125

BRADWELL BAY

One hundred and twenty-one aircrew were lost,
'who in answer to the call of duty,
left the airfield to fly into the blue forever'.

By 1942 the tide of the war was turning in the allies' favour and there was an increasing determination to take the fight to the enemy.

At the northern edge of the Dengie peninsular, at the mouth of the Blackwater estuary, stands the, now closed, Magnox nuclear power station. In 1942 this was the site of 'RAF Bradwell Bay' airfield, which became operational in April that year. The first arrivals at Bradwell were the Royal Canadian Air Force 418 squadron of twin-engine Boston aircraft painted in matt black. These aircraft were used as intruders for night operations over occupied Europe. Soon after, there followed a British mosquito squadron employed to attack specific enemy targets in France. As the war progressed many more squadrons came and went, or were rotated through, as the allies advanced after D Day. During the airfield's life, as well as British and Canadian, New Zealand, Australian and Czech pilots were based there. A whole variety of ancillary missions were undertaken, such as pathfinding, bomber escort and troop carrier support, the latter especially for the D-Day landings and the airborne landings at Arnhem in Holland. Of vital importance was the airfield's role in Air Sea Rescue. Returning aircraft were often forced to ditch in the sea. Sometimes they just ran out of fuel before reaching land. Homecoming Halifax and Lancaster bombers would also use Bradwell Bay as an emergency landing site because of its close proximity to the coast. The last operation from Bradwell was in April 1945 and the airfield closed completely in December that year.

Cast iron replica 'Mosquito'
memorial at Bradwell Bay

MULBERRY

Just over a mile offshore from Thorpe Bay, in the Thames estuary, are the remains of a 2,500 ton concrete Phoenix caisson partially sunk in the mud. It is a section of a Mulberry Harbour originally destined for use after the 'D' Day landings in World War Two. *Operation Overlord*, the invasion of Europe by 250,000 allied soldiers, took place on the 6th June 1944. It was an unprecedented logistical challenge. It was assumed that all the major French ports would be unusable which meant the allies needed to take their own harbours with them to support the landings and to re-supply the troops once ashore.

Many of the caissons were built in the docks on the River Thames although the River Colne based Wivenhoe Shipyard Ltd, already mentioned on page 125, constructed two of the tank landing buffers, codenamed 'whales', linking caissons to the tank landing pier.

Ariel view of the section of Mulberry harbour at Thorpe Bay

The D. Day plan was to tow the caissons to the site of the proposed harbour location on the Normandy coast and sink them in position. They would then serve as supports for the landing bridges.

Each concrete support caisson was hollow and if made watertight would float, although it is difficult to imagine concrete caissons weighing up to 5,000 tons bobbing about on the high seas.

The caisson resting in the River Thames was not made in Essex. It was one of six built in Goole dry docks, on the River Humber, by Henry Boot and Company. Classed as C1s these were the smallest of the caissons. One of them, while being moved south, sprang a leak off the River Crouch. It was towed into the Thames Estuary to await inspection but in a squall it broke free and ran aground. With the concrete shell punctured it flooded and at low tide it settled on a sandbank and broke in two.

Building the caissons was a huge task and undertaken in great secrecy. An apprentice, Frank Agar, who worked on the project for four months, commented that the workers had no idea what they were building. Some speculated they were concrete barges! Apart from the 500 people employed on building the six made in Goole another 6,000 worked on them in Essex. The name Mulberry was not significant, simply a code word for harbour. The concrete caissons were coded Phoenix. A fleet of ocean-going tugs towed them to Normandy. Two harbours were built, the first just off Arromanches, supporting the British and Canadian sector and the second at Omaha Beach for the Americans.

Operation Overlord was the largest seaborne invasion in history and began the process of liberating Nazi occupied Western Europe. Unlike the First World War, when there was no press reporting during the first weeks of the titanic Battle of the Somme, the *Essex Newsman* of 6th June 1944 devoted a full front page to the landings, headlined **'INVASION'**. The second battalion of the Essex Regiment, after their retreat from Dunkirk, returned to action in France on 7th June to take part in the liberation of Bayeux. A dedicated memorial to the 2nd Essex stands within Bayeux War Cemetery on the south-west of the town centre.

PILOTLESS AIRCRAFT

For more than a year the centre and south of Essex had been relatively free from enemy air attacks although both Clacton and Colchester suffered incendiary bombing in early 1944. Chelmsford suffered its last major raid in May 1943 when the town was targeted by nearly 100 bombers, in what was described as the Chelmsford blitz. Over 50 people were killed, including 11 patients at New Hall Hospital. Additionally 1,000 people were made homeless. As 'D' Day came closer, there was probably more danger to residents from either enemy aircraft being shot down or allied aircraft accidents. There were thousands of aircraft movements over Essex every day. With so much air traffic, crashes or collisions did occur, especially in bad weather. Added to this, several allied planes, damaged over enemy territory, limped home only to crash land before making it to the runway..

A V1 being made ready for launch somewhere in Northern France

A week after the D. Day landings, a new aerial threat materialised when the first V1 flying bombs hit London. Commonly known as Buzz Bombs or Doodlebugs, the official classification was PAC (Pilotless aircraft). These sub-sonic gyro guided planes could deliver a tonne of high explosive that went off on impact, causing huge material damage to buildings and homes in the vicinity.

On 16th June 1944, two V1s came down close to Boreham aerodrome although there were no reported casualties. The new menace caused another wave of evacuations. In all over 500 V1s came to ground in the county between June 1944 and March 1945, although towards the latter stages nearly 90% were shot down en-route to their target.

More worrying were the V2 rockets, ballistic missiles weighting 13 tons that travelled at speeds of up to 3,000 miles per hour. There were as yet no anti-aircraft guns or fighter planes capable of intercepting them. The only hope was for advancing allied forces on the continent to find and destroy the launching sites. As the enemy retreated the rocket batteries were withdrawn and the missiles could no longer reach London. As a consequence some 400 V2 rockets hit Essex. The worst single loss of life from a V2 in Essex took place on Tuesday 19th December 1944, when a rocket fell on Henry Road, near the Hoffman factory in Chelmsford, during a Christmas party. Thirty-nine people were killed and 138 injured, 47 seriously. Several dwellings in Henry Road were completely destroyed and many in nearby streets were badly damaged. The havoc and damage caused by pilotless aircraft caused the government to set an upper limit of £10.00 for the amount of repair work that could be done by an individual or firm without a special licence, with a maximum of figure of £100.00 per annum.

PRISONERS

During the Battle of Britain and the blitz that followed, a steady stream of German aircrew, who survived being shot down, became prisoners of war. Many were rescued from the waters round the Essex coastline. Captured aircrew were a regular sight in Southend. Nearly every day one of the trains to London from Shoeburyness had a carriage specially reserved for prisoners. After D. Day, as the allies advanced, the stream of captured enemy became a flood as huge numbers of German soldiers surrendered and were brought to the UK. At its peak there were about 400,000 POWs housed in the country in over 1,000 camps. At the time the government went to great pains to keep the actual numbers and locations secret and most of the contemporary records have since been destroyed. (By way of contrast the average prison population in the UK in 2015 was 79,000.)

Spread across Essex were 12 Prisoner of War (POW) camps including one each in the grounds of Hylands and Coronation Park near Chelmsford. The camps were identified by numbers which, for unknown reasons, were changed periodically. This often led to confusion, with different establishments having the same number. One of the biggest camps in the country was Number 186 Berechurch Camp, at Colchester. However there was also a camp designated 186 near Newport in Wales and when Berechurch closed another camp, number 260 at Fornham Hall near Bury St Edmunds, was changed to also become 186!

By April 1945, a month before the war in Europe ended, camp prisoner numbers were at their peak. Though in general camps didn't have watchtowers and few even had barbed wire fences, the majority of the inmates, realising that their war was lost, had no desire to escape. Berechurch was designed to hold 6,000 prisoners but at times numbers rose as high as 10,000, when prisoners in transit were being interrogated before being moved on. The first 1,500 POWs arrived in Colchester on the night of 19/20th September 1944. They were accommodated in 'twelve man' tents which in many cases they had to put up themselves. Within four days the camp was full. The winter was hard and by Christmas the fields were a quagmire. In February 1945 the first Nissen huts were erected and concrete roadways put down. Drainage and sanitation were considerably upgraded. Both had previously had been appalling. Soon, aided by a ready and enthusiastic POW workforce, Berechurch was a town within a town with over 1,300 semi-permanent buildings which included a hospital and a 200 seat theatre, where two theatre troupes and several choirs performed. The camp had a working farm, its own newspaper and two churches plus a catholic seminary, established so that priests who had been conscripted into the German Army could continue their religious studies.

In the west of Essex, camp number 116 was located in Mill Lane, Hatfield Heath. It initially housed Italian prisoners who were employed on local farms, helping with the harvest in the summer or ditch cleaning and hedge trimming in the winter. They were even allowed out to play football against the locals. A noted 'friendly' match against Hatfield Heath resulted in an 11-nil win for the prisoners.

Purfleet, on the River Thames, had three camps around Beacon Hill, numbers 286, 654 and 655. These accommodating 1000s of prisoners, many of whom stayed for just a short time before being moved elsewhere. Camp 266 was at Langdon Hills and could hold 800 prisoners. Again many of the men were sent to work on local farms or to help clear war damage.

Although the war in Europe ended on 8th May 1945, many of the prisoners were not repatriated for another three years. In many cases it was impractical to send them home as so much of the German infrastructure had been destroyed and there was no functioning government. Furthermore the prisoners were needed to work on the land to help clear war damage debris. There was an acute manpower shortage in Britain as it took months for British forces to return home from serving overseas. The authorities also wanted to be sure they had screened out any diehard Nazis so they wouldn't return to their homeland and cause further trouble.

Naturally many prisoners were desperate to go home as they had had no news of their families or hometown for years. Although no wartime breakouts were recorded at the Essex camps, there were two notable 'escapes' from Berechurch post war. The first, in February 1946, involved a group of prisoners who were performers in the camp theatre troupe. They objected to being instructed to work on the farm as it interfered with their rehearsals. Using their best acting skills about 20 cast members feigned sickness. Their performances were so convincing that the British medical officer agreed to them being sent home immediately, despite the fact that some actors had performed on stage every night for weeks. The other more bizarre escape was that of Private Hans Müller who was seconded to work on a farm near Ipswich. He managed to stow away on a ship bound for Hamburg. However, once in Germany, without identity papers (and no money to buy forged ones), life was almost impossible. From Hamburg he made his way to the Soviet sector of Berlin to see his mother. He was then arrested by the Russians but managed to escape after a few days. In frustration he made his way back to the coast and stowed away on a ship bound for Ipswich. From there he walked back to Berechurch. In August 1947, nearly a year after his departure he arrived back at the camp and asked the guards to let him back in. Berechurch Camp closed in September 1947. Hans Müller was subsequently released and given legitimate discharge papers, an identity card, a ration book and soon was on his way back home.

Once the prisoners had gone, some of the camps were used to house displaced families who had good reason not to return to their homeland, such as Austrians who had opposed the Nazis or Polish people who were now worried about the intentions of the Soviet Union in Poland. Today nearly all trace of the UK's World War II prison camps has been erased along with nearly all the records. Berechurch, however, has gained a new life as a, 'Military Corrective Training Centre'. It houses military prisoners detained from all three branches of the armed services.

Ariel view of Berechurch Camp in the 1980s

The War in Europe ended on 8th May 1945 (VE Day) and in Japan on 15th August (VJ) day. There were celebrations and street parties but many were muted. The county, as in the country at large, had an enormous job of reconstruction ahead of it. Nevertheless it was good news for the holiday resorts, for with the end of hostilities most made impressive efforts to reopen for the summer season. The *Essex Chronicle* reported that 10,000 people, one third of Chelmsford's population, were away in August, leaving the town deserted.

Perhaps the biggest post war shock came in the general election of July 1945. This resulted in the unexpected landslide victory for Clement Attlee's Labour Party and the defeat of the incumbent Winston Churchill. To date the 12.0% national swing from the Conservative Party to the Labour Party remains the largest ever achieved in a British general election.

ARMAGEDDON

Following the end of the Second World War the newly elected Labour Government had a multitude of problems to deal with. The nation was effectively bankrupt, there was an acute shortage of housing, fuel and vital foodstuffs so rationing had to continue. Nevertheless, the National Health Service was set up and the railways, power utilities and steel industry were nationalised.

In Europe, the Soviet Union, a vital ally in the fight against the Nazis, began to exert a tight grip on the nation states of Eastern Europe. This alarmed the United Kingdom, the United States and the liberated countries of Western Europe.

On March 5th 1946, barely nine months after Winston Churchill had failed to be re-elected as Prime Minister, whilst on a visit to the USA, he made a speech to Westminster College, Fulton, Missouri in which he said, 'From Stettin (in Poland) in the Baltic to Trieste in the Adriatic, an iron curtain has descended across the Continent'. The term 'Iron Curtain' heralded the beginning of the Cold War.

Tensions increased between the west and the Soviet Union when in 1948 the Soviets blockaded Berlin for the best part of a year. In August 1949 Russia conducted its first nuclear test and relations were further strained when in June 1950, together with China, it backed communist

North Korea's, invasion of South Korea. Within a few years, the Cold War nuclear arms race was at full steam.

As the nuclear stockpiles of the superpowers, Russia and America, grew the world trembled at the possibility that one of them would blink and Armageddon would ensue. Meanwhile in Essex, people were getting on with their lives oblivious to the fact that should this holocaust happen the county might be at the centre of dealing with the aftermath.

In the October 1951 general election, Winston Churchill was returned to office as Prime Minster. The Conservative party had a majority of 17 seats despite the Labour party polling a quarter of a million votes more. Almost a year later, officials from the War Office turned up at the Kelvedon Hatch farm of Jim Parrish with a compulsory purchase order for 25 acres of his land. This was the beginning of the 'Nuclear Bunker', the government's answer to nuclear bombardment!

Almost immediately, with military precision, public access to the site was banned, local roads were closed, the designated area was fenced off and patrols of armed guards were organised. The first contractor arrived to excavate a huge, deep hole. This was followed by a succession of builders all working under the cloak of the *Official Secrets Act*. Secrecy was paramount, each group completed its allocated task and left, not knowing what anyone else was doing or what the final objective of their labour was. Work carried on nonstop throughout the winter months, much of it in the dark. On completion of the bunker, the following March, the only visible result of all this work was a quite ordinary looking bungalow.

Underneath this innocent looking façade was a three-story bunker, a hundred feet deep and encased in walls of reinforced concrete, ten feet thick. With its entrance protected by steel blast proof doors, weighing one and half tons each, it was hoped that the bunker's occupants would survive the effects of a close proximity nuclear explosion.

Originally, at the start of the Cold War, a number of bunkers were built on the East Coast of Britain with the code name ROTOR. In each of them the Marconi Company installed the most up to date radar and communications equipment available and they were to serve as stations for the upgrading of air defences.

As tensions increased, the possibility of nuclear war began to loom. Plans to cope with the aftermath began to be made and the role of the bunker was changed. At a cost of £10 million the Kelvedon Hatch bunker was turned into a 'Regional Government Headquarters', with the code name RGHQ 5.1. In the event of nuclear attack, it was to be the control centre for London and the surrounding area. It would house 600 key personnel that would include top civil servants, cabinet ministers and even the Prime Minister of the day. The bunker was fully self-sufficient, with its own power supply as well as water and food for three months. There was also a 2,500-line telephone exchange and a BBC radio studio that could broadcast to the nation's survivors.

In order to educate the general public on how to prepare for a nuclear doomsday scenario a series of civil defence films were made. Most of these were never shown on the grounds that they might cause panic. Should the unthinkable happen, and nuclear attacks take place, scientists in the bunker would monitor fallout and radiation levels and advise on the risks. The prospects were bleak; it was assumed that millions of people would die, but millions would survive even though many might have a short life expectancy due to severe burns, radiation sickness and lack of medical attention, food and water. There was no provision to take family members into the bunker. The unit was to be protected by guards outside who would keep unwanted intruders out, and just as important, keep the key personnel in. Just how the guards were to survive is unclear!

Happily the bunker was never put to the ultimate test and the prospect of nuclear war faded. In 1989 the Berlin Wall came down, signalling the collapse of communism in Eastern Europe, and within two years the breakup of the Soviet Union was under way. With the Cold War effectively over the bunker was no longer needed. The £3 million annual running costs may have speeded up a decision by the government regarding its future. In December 1994 ownership of the land, together with the bunker, reverted to the original owners, the Parrish family. They decided to preserve the bunker as a reminder of what may have been.

Today, on the A128, between Brentwood and Ongar, prominent signs display directions to the 'Secret' Nuclear Bunker. It might be more accurate if the signs read; *This way to the Nuclear Bunker that is no longer secret'.* The bunker, once one of the most hush-hush buildings in the land, is now one of the more unusual tourist attractions in Essex.

During its 'operational' lifetime, when nuclear armageddon was a distinct possibility, there were just two ways to get in or out of the bunker - the entrance tunnel or the emergency stairs at the rear. With the Cold War over and since becoming a tourist 'attraction' a third exit has been added - on the grounds of health and safety!

Nuclear armageddon was a distinct possibility?

THE DAGENHAM LIGHT INFANTRY

At the time the Nuclear Bunker was being completed, the Korean War had been raging for three years. In April 1953, the 1st Battalion of the Essex Regiment, mainly comprised of national servicemen, received orders for deployment to Korea. With so many men coming from Dagenham the battalion quickly gained the nickname, 'The Dagenham Light Infantry'.

The fully equipped battalion left the UK in July 1953 on the troop ship *Asturias* for the month long sea voyage via the Suez Canal, Aden, Singapore and Hong Kong. However, as they neared the Korean peninsula, news was received that armistice talks had begun and combat had ceased. Nevertheless the battalion was instructed to continue to the port of Busan (formerly Pusan) disembarking there on 5th August. From Busan, they made their way overland 250 miles north to the demarcation line, roughly following the 38th parallel, that separated the opposing forces.

With no actual fighting in prospect the battalion was given two tasks, firstly the grim one of clearing the battlefield in their sector and secondly the work of strengthening what was known as the Kansas line, one of a series of secondary defensive positions set about five miles behind the front.

The Dagenham Boys. Home from Home

The Essex Battalion remained in Korea for 12 months during which time there was one casualty. On 16th June 1954 Private William Boreham was killed while attempting to dismantle an artillery shell. The following day the Battalion was withdrawn and returned to Busan for subsequent embarkation to their new posting in Hong Kong.

During their time away, the men overcame homesickness by putting up signposts pointing the way to familiar places. The illustration above shows a group of Dagenham men with their sign with arrows pointing towards Heathway, in Dagenham, and Ilford Broadway.

WINDS OF CHANGE

George VI, the king of the United Kingdom and the Dominions, was also the last Emperor of India and the first Head of the Commonwealth. He died on 6th February 1952, within weeks of the completion of the 'Secret Nuclear Bunker'. Elizabeth II ascended the throne at the age of 25. Her televised coronation, on 2nd June 1953 at Westminster Abbey, caused a surge in the sale of television sets. In April 1955, Prime Minister Winston Churchill, resigned due to ill health, and was replaced by Anthony Eden. A month later in a general election the Conservatives were returned with majority of 60.

Although memories of wartime shortages were fading fast, petrol rationing was reintroduced in December 1956 during the Suez crisis. In response to Egypt's nationalisation of the Suez Canal, Prime Minister Eden had authorised British forces to invade Egypt in conjunction with the French and Israelis. It was a political disaster and in January 1957 he resigned. He was replaced by Harold Macmillan who may be remembered for telling the British public 'you never had it so good'. He earned the nickname 'Supermac' for reviving the fortunes of his demoralised party and winning the 1959 election with an increased majority. On a visit to South Africa in 1960, Macmillan shocked his hosts in the Cape Town Parliament with;- *'The wind of change is blowing through this continent. Whether we like it or not, this growth of national consciousness is a political fact'*. He made it clear that where apartheid was in force there would be a shift in British policy.

The latter months of Macmillan's premiership were soured by the political scandal of the Profumo affair. He resigned due to ill health in October 1963 and was replaced by Sir Alec Douglas-Home.

During this period Essex had been largely peaceful, yet, in a holiday resort on the county's east coast, a battle, the like of which had not been seen before, was about to erupt! Macmillan's 'never had it so good' prosperity had created a new force in the land: 'Teenagers'; who had money in their pockets and the ability to travel as never before.

CLACTON'S EXPLOSIVE EASTER

The banner headline of Friday 3rd April 1964, spread across the front page of the *East Essex Gazette* read; **CLACTON COUNTS ITS LOSSES AFTER EASTER TEENAGE INVASION.**

Although the Easter weekend was cold and wet, the inclement weather didn't deter thousands of teenagers from travelling to Clacton. The newspaper described them as two distinct groups, those arriving on scooters and those riding on motorbikes.

In colourful language the *Gazette* described an unholy weekend of hoodlum inspired horror. Leather jacketed yobs had run amok with scenes reminiscent of the wild-west, in a 'terror-triangle' centred on Pier Avenue, Marine Parade and Agate Road. The chairman of the Clacton Guest House association spoke of his members being threatened by gangs roaming the streets. An old lady was reportedly thrown into a hedge and guests were abused in their hotels. One hotelier reported dozens of ruffians breaking into his premises, rampaging around and stealing blankets. A town centre coach operator reported boys and girls smashing open parked vehicles sleeping in them overnight and then leaving them in a filthy mess with seats ripped up and fittings damaged. Clacton airstrip, which had been used as camping ground, was left covered in fish and chip papers, milk cartons, empty beer bottles and broken glass. The bowling club was broken into, its interior wrecked and the bar stripped.

Takings in bars, cafes and restaurants over the weekend had tumbled. Many businesses, as well as residents, blamed the Clacton Council for not doing enough to curb the violence and threatened to withhold payment of their rates. More serious though were the threats to the economic future of the town. Delegates to the 750 strong Co-operative weekend conference, whose proceeding were disrupted, said they would ensure that the society would never choose Clacton again.

The following Wednesday, Clacton Council met under the chair of Councillor D. H. R. Moody. The surveyors department confirmed widespread damage to plate glass windows, beach shelters and seating. Both of the town's beach inspectors, Messrs Page and Freeman, reported being assaulted near the pier and said that a mob had thrown glasses, shovels and chairs into the children's boating lake.

Superintendent Wood, addressing the council, said that police reinforcements had been called in from all over Essex to deal with problems. The trouble was caused by some 800 males and 300-400 females of which sixty, aged between 15 and 22, had been arrested in the town. He was quoted as saying that the youth of the country should have it impressed upon them that they were not the important people they believed themselves to be. He added that industry pandered to them by selling them pop records, fancy clothes and beat music. The culprits were not normal teenagers, but the lowest forms of humanity, and he was of the opinion that they hadn't had a wash since arriving. All they wanted to do was to scorch around on scooters and get in people's hair.

Councillor D. Nicolls said that if she had the power she would deport the offenders to Alaska for six months. Councillor Payne suggested the formation of a Clacton vigilantes group to deter any trouble over the forthcoming Whitsun weekend. Nothing much came of this suggestion. However, Clacton led the way in forming a nationwide 'Stop-the-Thugs' campaign.

Councillor Moody complained that although what happened was serious, the events of the Easter Weekend had been wildly exaggerated by the national press. He said he had received calls from Paris and Washington about the 'riots' in Clacton and the 'troubles' were reported on the front pages of Hong Kong's *China Mail* and Florida's *Orlando Evening Star*.

The letters column of the *Gazette* was full of angry correspondence about the disturbances, including one signed by 'DISGUSTED RATEPAYER' who wrote; '...the ostrich like tactics of the council were responsible for failing to curb the trouble'. The local Member of Parliament, Mr Julian Ridsdale, took up the matter with the Home Secretary who in turn promised everything possible would be done to ensure that there was no recurrence of the hooliganism. A month later Clacton Court was busy handing out fines and detention terms for a variety of offences, including assault, being drunk and disorderly, theft, vandalism and obtaining credit by fraud.

The *Gazette* had not used the term *Mods* and *Rockers* in the context of the Clacton disturbances, although it went to the trouble of finding two local youths to dress up and pose for pictures in front of their respective scooter or motorcycle to illustrate the identity of each group; the 'Mods', in their fashionable suits and 'Parkas', and the 'Rockers' with their long hair and motor cycling leathers.

Much to the relief of Clacton's residents, the Whitsun weekend of 1964 passed off relatively peacefully. Instead the *Mods* and *Rockers* descended upon Margate, Brighton or Southend, where they attacked each other, in the process causing mayhem and inflicting damage on the resorts.

In 1979 the film *Quadrophenia* was released telling the story of a London based *Mod* who escaped from a dead-end job and rode his scooter to Brighton where he brawled with the motorcycle-riding *Rockers*.

THE BATTLE OF THE AIRWAVES
PIRATES

During a force eight gale, on Wednesday January 19th 1966, the *Mi Amigo*, a converted cargo boat and home of the 'pirate' radio station, *Radio Caroline*, was swept ashore at Frinton-on-Sea near Walton-on-the-Naze. Hours earlier it had been broadcasting from an anchorage just beyond British territorial waters.

Maybe it was prophetic but the number two song on *Radio Caroline's* chart that week was 'My Ship is Coming in' by the Walker Brothers. The crew and DJs, who included Tony Blackburn and Dave Lee Travis, were taken to Walton-on-the-Naze police station where, classed as 'shipwrecked and distressed mariners', they were given free replacement clothing.

Radio Caroline had begun broadcasting nearly two years earlier when DJ Simon Dee, aboard the Motor Vessel *Fredrica* (the predecessor of the *Mi Amigo*), uttered the following words; 'Hello everybody. This is *Radio Caroline*, broadcasting on 199, your all-day music station'. These words became inseparable from the so called 'swinging sixties'.

It was not on a whim that the first offshore stations were moored off the Essex coast. With their powerful transmitters they were strategically placed to reach audiences in London, East Anglia and the Midlands. In spite of government threats and efforts at discouragement, millions of people tuned in to these new broadcasters. *Radio London* quickly joined *Caroline*, and then *Radio England, Britain Radio* and even a *Radio Essex* took to the airwaves. Soon the waters off Essex were crowded with 'wannabee' broadcasters.

Today it is difficult to imagine what little choice listeners had then in the way of broadcast music. Prior to the arrival of *Caroline*, what now is classed as pop music was only continuously available from foreign stations such *Radio Luxembourg*, which tended to fade out at night, or *Radio Veronica*, a Dutch 'pirate' anchored off the coast of Holland.

Radio Veronica's transmissions were aimed at a Dutch audience, consequently its language was Dutch, although most of the music played was English and American from the popular charts of the day. Even so its broadcasts could be heard over much of Eastern England and provided a stark contrast to the dull music offerings available from the BBC Light Programme.

Today the 60s 'Radio Pirates' are remembered with a degree of rose tinted nostalgia. Many of the first offshore personalities went on to become respected in the 'legal' broadcasting profession or achieved success in other walks of life. Yet the British governments of the day, whether Conservative or Labour, strongly opposed 'pirate' broadcasting. They cited interference with the safety of shipping and emergency wavebands as well as perceived harmful or subversive effects on the population at large. In 1965 Edward Short, the Postmaster General, who had responsibility for broadcasting, said the offshore radio stations were 'squalid enterprises akin to burglars'.

The government issued threats of action against illegal activity on the high seas but did little to enforce them. It was left to the weather to do the job for them. Although *Mi Amigo* had been washed ashore, and the people aboard were lucky to have survived, *Radio Caroline* was back on the air within two months. Despite this the days of the 'pirates' were numbered.

The experience of the *Mi Amigo* highlighted the vulnerability to the weather of ship based pirate stations. To avoid this some broadcasters set their sights on the disused war time forts that were scattered around the Essex coast and the Thames Estuary. These were solid in construction and, fortunately for the pirates, just outside territorial waters.

One such fort was *Shivering Sands,* (see opposite) located roughly midway between Essex and Kent, in the Thames estuary. It was occupied in the summer of 1964 by Reg Calvert, a music promoter from the West Midlands, together with performer and singer, David (Screaming Lord) Sutch. David Sutch naturally wanted to get his music played to the widest possible audience but the BBC had rejected his records as unsuitable. Consequently *Radio Sutch* was born.

Whilst Reg Calvert and David Sutch had a flair for self-promotion, neither had the expertise nor the proper resources to run a radio station. *Radio Sutch* used cobbled together equipment that worked erratically. Living conditions on the fort were rudimentary and the station's broadcasts were so weak that they only attracted a tiny audience. The programmes themselves were put together piecemeal and the lack of revenue became critical as there was no income from advertising. After a few months David Sutch tired of living on an old war time fort and moved on and *Radio Sutch* vanished from the airwaves.

Reg Calvert had other ideas. He was determined that his radio enterprise would succeed. Stronger second hand transmitters were obtained and *Radio Sutch* was replaced by the grandiosely named *'Radio City - The Tower of Power'*. Yet this station was tiny compared to the main offshore broadcasters like *Caroline* or *Radio London*.

Shivering Sands. Midway between Essex and Kent and outside territorial waters?

Nevertheless, Shivering Sands was an attractive proposition to the ship based broadcasters. In September 1965, merger talks began between Reg Calvert's *Radio City* and *Radio Caroline South*, operated by a company called Project Atlanta. It was proposed that the new operation be based on Shivering Sands and that the *Mi Amigo*, Caroline's base, be scrapped. During the negotiations *Radio City* attempted to take delivery of new transmitters but, in the course of unloading, one of the heavy cabinets fell into the sea. Although it was recovered with the help of local divers, it was judged to be useless.

Unfortunately for Reg Calvert his woes were compounded when Project Atlanta went bust and *Mi Amigo* and *Radio Caroline South* were taken over by Ronan O'Rahilly, the original founder of *Radio Caroline*. Reg Calvert then began talks with *Radio London* and it seemed a deal could be done. The Chairman of the defunct Project Atlanta was Major Oliver Smedley, a former paratrooper. He had been responsible for buying the transmitter that had fallen into the sea and, as far as he was concerned, it belonged to him. He concluded that should a *Radio City/London* merger go through he would lose out.

The Major decided to act in the best way he knew and, along with his co-investor Kitty Black, a London West End impresario, he organised a raiding party made up of steel riggers. On 21st June 1966, Shivering Sands was seized by Smedley under the cover of darkness and transmissions were shut down. The DJs and engineers were confined to their quarters. Having secured their objective, Smedley and Kitty Black left for the mainland, leaving the steel riggers in charge of the fort along with their assorted 'prisoners' under the command of 'Big' Alf Bullen.

The seizure of the fort made national headlines. Reg Calvert was outraged and rushed to the village of Wendens Ambo near Saffron Walden to confront Oliver Smedley at his home. Arriving around 11pm, Calvert reportedly forced his way past the housekeeper. During the course of a heated argument Smedley produced a shotgun and Reg Calvert was shot dead.

In October 1966 Oliver Smedley's trial for manslaughter opened at Chelmsford Assizes. The charge had already been reduced from murder. Smedley claimed self-defence. The jury took less than two minutes to return a verdict of not guilty. Mr Justice Melford Stevenson then awarded Smedley 250 guineas costs.

In February 1967, Dorothy, the widow of Reg Calvert, and Managing Director of Radio City, appeared at Rochford Magistrates Court charged with violating the Wireless Telegraphy Act of 1949. A new government marine survey had determined that Shivering Sands fort was in fact inside UK territorial limits, even though seven months earlier it had been deemed to be outside! Mrs Calvert was found guilty and fined £100.00. Radio City closed immediately.

The seizure of Shivering Sands, the killing of Reg Calvert, the subsequent trial and events surrounding it had far reaching implications. The Labour Government, newly returned to office with a substantially increased majority under Harold Wilson, felt justified in asserting that pirate radio was being run by gangsters and tax dodgers. Draft legislation to outlaw offshore radio was speedily brought onto the statute book. With the passing of the August 1967 Marine Offences Act, all the offshore stations except *Radio Caroline* shut down.

The government had won its battle with the pirates but to appease the listening public the BBC launched Radio 1 which began broadcasting on Saturday 30th September 1967 with none other than Tony Blackburn at the helm.

In defiance of the new law, *Radio Caroline* continued to broadcast intermittently from the *Mi Amigo*. However, in March 1980 during a storm, the 60 year old ship, which by then was barely seaworthy, sank after running aground on the Long Sand Bank south of Clacton-on-Sea. The crew were all taken off unharmed. Two years later *Radio Caroline* was resurrected and began transmitting from a new vessel, the converted trawler *Ross Revenge*. In November 1991 this too was abandoned during a gale and ran aground on the Goodwin Sands. Unlike the *Mi Amigo*, it was later salvaged and restored in Tilbury Docks. The *Ross Revenge* is now moored in the River Blackwater. *Radio Caroline* is no longer a 'pirate'. The station broadcasts completely legally and can be heard via satellite and online. In May 2017 the broadcast regulator OFCOM awarded *Radio Caroline* a licence to broadcast on AM from the *Ross Revenge*. At the time of writing the frequency has not been allocated.

The battle against radio pirates still continues though. In March 2012 illegal radio broadcasting equipment was seized from the top of a tower block in Havering. A transmitter was found concealed in a ventilation shaft connected to the power supply in a lift motor room.

The Times reported 150 land based 'pirate' radio stations were broadcasting and speculated that one third of them were run by criminal gangs that played music that glamourised gun and drug culture. It was said that some drug dealers would tune in to wait for a coded message or for a particular song to be played, knowing that would be a signal that their next shipment was ready for collection.

The language from parliament today is much the same as in the sixties. References to modern day pirate radio stations have included them being described as, 'a living embodiment of contempt for the law that harms local communities with a wanton disregard of the health and safety of others'. The battle goes on!

THE PENTONVILLE FIVE
The Battle of Chobham Farm

In June 1970, Harold Wilson's Labour Party lost the General Election and the Conservatives, under Edward Heath, were returned to office. It was the first election in which people could vote from the age of 18. Prime Minister Heath is remembered for two things, taking the United Kingdom into the Common Market, the forerunner of the European Union, and chaotic industrial relations that culminated in the miners' strike, power blackouts and the three day week.

One could be forgiven for thinking that Chobham Manor was a grand stately home, perhaps somewhere near the village of Chobham near Woking. In fact Chobham Manor is the name given to a new neighbourhood in Stratford, on the eastern part of the Olympic Park site, and is part of the legacy of the 2012 London Games (on the western border of the old metropolitan Essex). The development also occupies the site of a battle that, in the 1970s, profoundly changed the course of industrial relations in Britain. Its name comes from the long forgotten 'Chobham Farm'.

Stratford has had a Chobham Road for at least 150 years. It runs west from the Leytonstone Road towards what was once Chobham Farm. Although the farm disappeared during the late 19th century, the name stuck despite the industrialisation of the River Lea valley and the expansion of Great Eastern Railway's works at Temple Mills. By the 1960s, Chobham Farm was just a quaint place name for an industrial estate where storage and distribution were the main businesses.

In July 1972, one of these businesses, Midland Cold Storage Ltd, became the centre of an industrial dispute of epic proportions. The dispute unfolded against the backdrop of the ongoing impasse between the trade union movement and the Conservative Government of Edward Heath that was marked by ugly clashes and mass picketing.

At this time the London Docks were rapidly losing business, mainly due to their inability to accommodate the ever increasing size of cargo ships. The main bone of contention for dockworkers though was the advent of containerisation. This enabled freight to be unloaded straight from ships onto trucks or railway wagons with a fraction of the existing dockside labour, since containers could be packed or unpacked away from the docks by anyone. To minimise job losses, a complex agreement was reached between the unions and the employers that obliged businesses within five miles of any dock to use only registered dockworkers to pack and unload containers.

Midland Cold Storage Ltd, although located only two miles from the Royal Docks, refused to recognise the agreement and chose not to employ dockers at their container depot at Chobham Farm. As a consequence they were targeted by mass pickets in an attempt to stop them trading. After eight weeks the picketing was having the desired effect. The company was suffering and its directors applied to the newly formed National Industrial Relations Court (NIRC) for an injunction to halt the picketing. The injunction was granted yet, in spite of this, the picketing continued.

In an effort to resolve the situation the company employed private investigators to infiltrate the protesters. Subsequently five shop stewards from the Transport and General Workers Union were

WARNING
THIS
DEPOT
IS
DOCK WORK
KEEP
OUT

A sign warning non-dockworkers to keep away

identified as pickets. Warrants were issued by the court for their arrest on charges of contempt. On 21st July 1972 the five; Bernie Steer, Vic Turner, Derek Watkins, Cornelius Clancy and Anthony Merrick, were arrested and taken to Pentonville Prison. From that day they became known as 'The Pentonville Five'.

The arrests and imprisonment led to outrage in union circles. There followed a series of rolling strikes and work stoppages that amounted to a general strike in all but name. On July 25th thousands of striking workers; dockers, builders, newspapermen, brewery and post office workers to name but a few, marched in protest through North London to Pentonville Prison. The Trades Union Congress (TUC) demanded the release of the five shop stewards and called an official national strike on 31st July.

The government seemed powerless to act and stalemate ensued. Then, to everyone's surprise, salvation came in the shape of Norman Turner, the Official Solicitor. One of the functions of this little known court official was to represent those unable to represent their own interests. He successfully applied to the Court of Appeal for the release of the five, on the grounds that the National Industrial Relations Court had insufficient grounds to deprive them of their liberty and that the evidence of the private investigators was flawed. The day after the protest march, 26th July, the arrest warrants were overturned.

The five shop stewards were released and a constitutional crisis in the making had been averted. Harold Wilson, then leader of the opposition, commented 'the government had been saved by a fairy godmother'. After another eighteen months of industrial strife, power cuts and the infamous three day week the Prime Minister, Edward Heath, called an election in February 1974, and was defeated.

One of the first actions of Harold Wilson's Labour government was to introduce the, 'Trade Union and Labour Relations Act', which abolished the National Industrial Relations Court. The NIRC had been established by the Conservative administration primarily as a way to limit the power of the trade unions. In its short life its perceived bias against the unions was a continuous source of controversy in labour circles, with most unions refusing to cooperate with it. The events at Chobham farm and the arrest and rapid release of the five shop stewards certainly hastened its demise. A battle had been won yet the war in the docks was unwinnable. Despite all the protests, and the temporary euphoria at the release of the Pentonville Five, the dock labour force inexorably declined. A worldwide revolution in the use of containerisation was unstoppable. Within ten years all the London docks had closed as major cargo handling centres.

The Pentonville Five went their separate ways, although each retained their strong union links. Victor Turner, who returned to work at the Royal Docks and later Tilbury docks, in 1984 was elected to Newham Borough Council and in 1997/8 served as Mayor of Newham. During this period he was also presented with the Transport and General Workers Union Gold Medal for his union work. Turner retired from the council in 2006 and died on 30th December 2012.

Political uncertainty continued and in February 1974 Edward Heath called a snap election which resulted in a hung parliament; the Labour party won most seats but not enough for an overall majority. Heath resigned and Harold Wilson became Prime Minister for a second time. He called a second election in October and gained an overall majority of just three seats. Resigning unexpectedly in March 1976, Wilson was replaced by Jim Callaghan. Meanwhile the Conservative party ousted Edward Heath as leader and elected Margaret Thatcher.

Callaghan's years in office were dogged by troubles. With such a small majority the government had to constantly do deals with smaller parties to keep the government functioning. Against a background of rising inflation and unemployment, and a seemingly never ending stream of industrial disputes, the government's problems mounted culminating in what became known as 'The Winter of Discontent'.

The most notorious action in the winter of 1978/1979 was by striking cemetery workers in Liverpool who refused to bury dead bodies. Funeral corteges were halted by pickets at cemetery gates and forced to turn back. Over 300 bodies were left piled in a cold storage depot and the council even discussed the possibility of burial at sea. Further south, striking refuse collectors caused huge piles of rotting uncollected rubbish, frequently overrun with rats, to accumulate in the centre of London and become a serious health hazard. The government's ordinary work ground to a halt.

Faced with increasing problems at every turn, in March 1979 James Callaghan lost a motion of no confidence in the House of Commons and in the May election the Conservatives were returned to office under the premiership of Margaret Thatcher. Amongst her election promises, Mrs Thatcher pledged to bring order to the chaotic industrial relations gripping the country.

THE ENEMY WITHIN

In the 1983 election Margaret Thatcher led the Conservatives to victory with an increased majority, attributed in part to the successful outcome of the Falklands War. However, the state of industrial relations in the country was still parlous and nowhere more so than in the coal mining industry.

In March 1984 the men at Cortonwood Colliery, Yorkshire walked out following notice of its closure. Within a few days, nearly half of all mining's 180,000 workforce were on strike. Arthur Scargill, the president of the National Union of Mineworkers, called on the N.U.M. to make the strike official. The miners' objective was to cause a severe energy shortage, and force the government to repeal planned closures. They hoped to repeat the success achieved against the Heath government 10 years earlier.

Whilst there were no coal mines in Essex, there were a number of small non-unionised ports on the River Colne, close to Colchester, where imported coal could be unloaded. Since widespread picketing was causing severe disruption within the coal fields and at the traditional ports, Brightlingsea, Wivenhoe and Hythe became scenes of intense activity. Queues of freighters, carrying imported coal, lined up in the River Colne to be unloaded round the clock from the end of March and through the summer months of 1984.

The Thatcher government's strategy was designed with a threefold objective; to keep as many mines working as possible, to increase and maintain adequate coal stocks with imports and to use the police to break up, or prevent, picketing. The first recorded incident of this in Essex was of Kentish miners travelling north to support the strike. They were intercepted at the Dartford Tunnel by a large police contingent and threatened with arrest if they continued.

The enemy within?

In late March a vanguard of Kent miners arrived in Colchester to assess the situation in Essex. Having had reports of coal being imported locally they sought support from local unions and accommodation for picketing miners. By April fifty men from Kent were billeted in the area. After discussing tactics, Wivenhoe port was selected as their first target.

To begin with all was peaceful. In mid-April a contingent of Welsh miners arrived to reinforce the Kent men and the first arrests occurred, immediately followed by allegations of police brutality.

As more strikers arrived in Essex to picket, the police mounted a huge surveillance operation to identify them and find out where they were staying. Some were in student accommodation at the University of Essex. Once identified, their movements and who they met was monitored. At the same time the police set up a tactical command headquarters in Wivenhoe football ground and were building up a database of car registration numbers in order to track vehicle movements.

In turn the miners, with more men on the ground, began picketing the other Essex ports and wharves including Mistley, further north on the River Stour.

To stop the miners moving around the police started setting up road blocks. One of these was a round the clock operation on Colchester's Greenstead roundabout, which links St Andrew's Avenue, Avon Way, Clingoe Hill and the A134 to Wivenhoe and Brightlingsea. This was a strategic point where the police could intercept pickets and detain them on suspicion that they would breach the peace later. The miners, unsurprisingly, described the action as harassment.

The dispute dragged on throughout May and June. In July the Prime Minister made a speech to the 1922 back bench committee where she referred to the coal strike, in its 19th week, as being instigated without a ballot. She said we had witnessed an unprecedented scale of violence and intimidation on the picket lines and that the nation must stand firm and militancy must not win. Controversially Mrs Thatcher added, 'We had to fight the enemy without in the Falklands. We always have to be aware of the enemy within, which is much more difficult to fight and more dangerous to liberty'.

'The enemy within' was taken as a, none too subtle, reference to the miners' leaders and their supporters in the labour movement. In September 1984, the High Court ruled the strike illegal as no national ballot had been held. Despite this the leadership ordered the strike to continue and in turn the union funds were sequestered.

During the strike 204 arrests were made in and around Colchester, mainly for obstruction, breach of the peace and threatening behaviour. Twenty nine men were taken into custody on what the police described as preventive detention. The more serious cases were tried in January and April 1985 at Chelmsford Crown Court. One Kent miner, convicted of 'Grievous Bodily Harm', was sentenced to five years in prison. Five others received three year jail terms after being convicted of arson at a haulage yard in Ardleigh, north of Colchester. The cost of the strike to the Essex ratepayer was enormous although the final figures were never made clear. However, after only two months into the strike, the bill for policing the picketing in Essex was already estimated at over £1 million.

The strike ended on 3rd March 1985 after most of the strikers had returned to work. The union had failed to stop coal reaching power stations or to get any more than token support from other unions. The critical element was seen as the NUM's failure to hold a strike ballot, which enabled a significant minority to keep working, which in turn kept other unions from supporting it.

In 1983 Britain had 174 working pits. Today there are none. Margaret Thatcher remained as British Prime Minister until 1990. She was the longest-serving British prime minister of the 20th century and the first woman to have held the office. After a bruising internal battle in the Conservative party, she was replaced by John Major as party leader and Prime Minister.

John Major, much to the surprise of most commentators, went on to win a fourth successive term for the Conservative party in the 1992 election. His premiership was dogged by internal party divisions, especially over Europe and his government became embroiled in a succession of 'sleaze' scandals involving Members of Parliament and Cabinet Ministers.

All had been relatively quiet in the county of Essex since the miner's strike just over ten years previously but this was about to change. The tranquillity of the River Colne estuary was about to be disturbed again.

LAMBS TO THE SLAUGHTER
(The Battle of Brightlingsea 1995)

The phrase *'The Battle of Brightlingsea'* was coined by the *Independent* newspaper, in its reporting of a series of protests held in Brightlingsea, between 16th January – 30th October 1995, against the export of livestock from the port. The name was used after Essex Police used riot control measures against demonstrators.

At the centre of the conflict was the export of live animals to the continent, especially lambs and veal calves. A growing, and increasingly militant, animal rights movement was completely opposed to it and the conditions in which the animals were transported. Numerous cases had been reported of harsh treatment of animals on long journeys. In one notorious example of 400 sheep shipped to Greece, 300 had died from heat exhaustion. Incidents like this caused outrage. Opposition to the trade grew from the general public staunchly backed-up by some celebrities and members of parliament.

The trade had been going on for years at other ports but with increasing difficulty for exporters. By 1995, the public had become increasingly concerned about the conditions in which animals were transported. The two largest campaign groups, Compassion in World Farming (CIWF) and the RSPCA, had called for a ban on all live exports. In other parts of the country ports at Shoreham in Sussex, Plymouth in Devon and Kings Lynn in Norfolk had already ceased shipments after furious demonstrations over the suffering of sheep and cattle packed into huge transport vehicles for excessive periods.

As a result, Brightlingsea, a quiet Essex port, became the location of a showdown. Determined live animal exporters Richard Otley of Cambridge and Roger Mills of Suffolk came together with an amenable port owner, Ernest Oliver of Brightlingsea docks to continue their business. After all, Parliament had deemed, even allowing that the welfare of animals was paramount, that the trade was lawful.

Matters came to head on 16th January 1995. Protesters, largely local residents, including school children, their parents and grandparents, under the auspices of BALE (Brightlingsea Against Live Exports) set up a cordon on the Colne Road to stop vehicles carrying livestock entering the port. Late in the day, one lorry carrying 400 sheep arrived escorted by a police van. However the demonstrators, by then swollen to a thousand, far outnumbered the police and on the grounds of safety the lorry was turned round. Yet this was just the first day, and the protesters' victory was short lived. Two days later 250 police officers, kitted out in full riot gear, arrived, determined to ensure that the Queen's highway would no longer be blocked and the animal cargoes would make it to the port.

During the course of the following ten months, 174 convoys carrying 150,000 sheep and 60,000 veal calves arrived in Brightlingsea. The animals were shipped to Belgium on the *MV Caroline*, a vessel that could negotiate the shallow depth of the river Colne. (There is no connection with the pirate radio station of the same name.)

Throughout the spring and summer demonstrators, often numbering thousands, did their best to halt the shipments. Brightlingsea became the focus of national and international media attention. On occasions the demonstrations turned violent as tempers were lost. The ranks of the protesters, largely peaceful but vociferous, were swollen at times by agitators whose sole purpose was to cause trouble and violence. In their turn the police were frequently accused of heavy handedness.

During the ten months of protests one man died, 598 people were arrested and 1,200 complaints were made against the police. Thousands of pounds worth of damage was inflicted on the port area and policing costs were estimated in millions of pounds. Whilst the physical damage could be repaired quickly it would take much longer for the psychological scars to heal. Such was the emotional intensity of the protest that many protesters suffered broken marriages, lost their jobs or even had their businesses ruined.

At times the police invoked the public order act and several injunctions were taken out by the exporters against leading protesters. The injunctions were eventually thrown out by the High Court. The protesters were fortunate in having Gerry Backhouse, who lived locally, to advise them in combating the actions of the exporters as well as those of the authorities. As a former MI5 spy during the Cold War, he was able to spot what might be termed 'dirty tricks' and propose effective responses. It was on his advice that, as a precaution, to prevent legal action against the organisation, BALE was temporarily disbanded.

The protests continued until Monday 30th October 1995 when suddenly shipments ended. Roger Mills announced that, due to the high costs and chaos caused by the protests at Brightlingsea, he would be transferring operations to Dover.

In the aftermath numerous court cases were heard. The Assistant Chief Constable of Essex was charged with breaking the Colne Road by-laws but was cleared at the court hearing. The exporter, Roger Mills, was convicted of dangerous driving and banned, having been accused of running down a protester, but this was overturned on appeal. However, he was later fined a substantial amount after being found guilty of failing to keep sheep in proper conditions. Ernest Otley, the Port Owner, was fined having been found guilty of threatening behaviour. Most of the complaints against the police were quashed and two protesters accused of assaulting a police officer were cleared and subsequently received a large out of court settlement.

There appeared to be few winners in the dispute except perhaps one. A sheep was 'kidnapped' from the port by protesters and christened 'Lucky the Lamb'. Lucky never went to Belgium and presumably survived to a ripe old age in an unknown location. In practice, the export of live animals continued from other ports, halting only in February 1996 when the European Union banned live exports from Britain over fears of 'mad cow disease' entering the European food chain.

Which one was Lucky? The One That Got Away

John Major and the Conservative Government were resoundingly defeated in the General Election of 1997 in one of the largest electoral defeats in over 150 years. The Labour Party was returned to office led by Tony Blair who, at 43, had the distinction of becoming the youngest Prime Minister since Lord Liverpool in 1812. He went on to win three successive elections, but resigned in 2007 and was replaced by Gordon Brown. For the Labour party Blair had proved to be a winner but his legacy remains mired in controversy due to his unwavering support for the US led invasion of Iraq in 2003. Gordon Brown remained as Prime Minster until May 2010 when the election resulted in a hung parliament.

David Cameron duly took office as Prime Minister on the 11th May 2010. The Conservatives were supported by the Liberal Democrats ushering in the first peacetime coalition for 100 years.

THE BATTLE OF DALE FARM

Since the 1970s, the travelling life styles of the nomadic community of English and Irish gypsies of Romany descent, lately swollen by groups of seemingly rootless new age travellers, had come under scrutiny. With ever rising property prices creating an acute shortage of land their traditional resting sites had become fewer, leading to demands that sites be provided for them. When sites were designated, this in turn led to increasing hostility from the settled community. A resolution was required and the government decided it was time to act. In Essex, Basildon became a focal point.

The *Battle of Dale Farm* reached its climax at 7am on 19th October 2011, when the clearance of this travellers' encampment began. The camp had been judged illegal and a court order had been issued. This authorised the forced removal of around 400 residents including about 100 children. Electricity had been disconnected earlier.

While three helicopters monitored events from above, one hundred and fifty police officers in full riot gear broke through the back fence of the encampment. As the police moved in they were pelted with rocks, lumps of wood and sprayed with an unknown powder.

One person was tasered and a caravan was set ablaze. Police intelligence had suggested that the site was packed with booby traps, gas canisters, petrol and nail bombs, and that some of the occupants had access to guns. Several threats of physical violence were made against the bailiffs who followed half an hour later to begin dismantling illegal structures.

Final eviction

Although some of the residents left voluntarily the numbers in the camp had grown as they had been swelled by outside supporters who were determined to stay put. The police met the strongest resistance at the front gate of the site where a 12-metre high scaffold tower was the centre piece of the defences. The battle with the police continued into the following day until the last demonstrators were removed from this structure. By the afternoon of 20th October the police had gained full control and the remaining residents walked out.

The battle of Dale Farm was brought vividly to life through minute by minute updates on social media. The forced eviction was front page news in both local and national newspapers and dramatic pictures were relayed around the world via the international press.

Essex Police stated that during the two day operation there had been 34 arrests for offences which included violent disorder, breach of the peace and obstruction.

A demonstrator being removed from the 12-metre high scaffold tower

All those arrested were described as 'activists' and not site residents. Half a dozen people were taken to hospital with minor injuries. The site was thoroughly searched. No guns, petrol, nail bombs or booby traps were found, although two wheelie bins packed with rocks were discovered at the back of the site.

The events of 19/20th October were the culmination of a ten year legal tussle between Basildon District Council and the 'travelling' residents of Dale Farm. At its height Dale Farm, along with the adjacent, and legal, Oak Lane site, housed over 1,000 people, the largest traveller concentration in the UK and possibly in Europe.

The disputed site, a rectangular shaped plot measuring approximately 500 yards long by 200 yards wide is set back from the north side of the A127 Southend arterial road. Obscured by trees, it lies about a mile south of Crays Hill. The area had been subject to green belt controls since 1982. About half of the area, known as the Oak Lane site, had previously gained Council planning permission for a traveller's site with 34 pitches. The other half, known as Dale Farm, was home to a scrap dealer, Ray Bocking. His house was on seven and half acres of land leased from Basildon Council in the 1960s.

Over time his 'green' fields had been concreted over and used as a scrap yard and dump but without planning permission. In 2001 an enforcement order to quit was served on Bocking. He in turn sold Dale Farm to a family of Irish travellers.

As a consequence of the acute shortage of land in urban areas, planning permission for traveller's sites became more and more difficult to obtain. Matters were also exacerbated by some travellers purchasing green field sites and building on them, in contravention of the all planning rules, in the hope of permission being granted retrospectively.

The development of Dale Farm followed this pattern. The new owners cleared the site of scrap and were joined by other travellers, to the consternation of Basildon District Council, local residents and the Member of Parliament. From the council's point of view once a settlement was established, no matter how illegally, the problems of eviction were much greater as there would be children's welfare and a host of social and health issues to be taken into account. The council explored all legal avenues. Numerous injunctions were issued only to be frequently overturned on appeal and eviction orders were continually subject to judicial review.

In the meantime the government began the slow process of tightening the law. The travellers had support in Parliament and were backed by numerous human rights, welfare, and artistic groups and even the United Nations and the Red Cross. To try and resolve the dilemma Basildon Council offered alternative 'bricks and mortar' accommodation but this was rejected by the travellers as being alien to their lifestyle.

The Dale Farm travellers themselves were not united on what were the best tactics. Many preferred to continue the legal route whilst others wanted engage in active resistance. With all the publicity Dale Farm became a 'cause célèbre' and attracted 'activists' from all over Europe. The arrival of outside activists worsened tensions within the Dale Farm community; they effectively took over the role of active resistance making the site a fortified encampment. In early October 2011 the final legal hurdle was overcome and the scene was set for the final showdown. It then became a waiting game as to when the eviction process would begin.

Although technically the eviction went smoothly, it didn't solve the problem. Many of the Dale Farm residents simply moved their caravans on to Oak Lane itself as opposed to pitches on the legal site. Some travellers did leave the area only to return after being evicted from their new destination. Basildon Council then began serving eviction notices on caravans packed on the local roads.

By Christmas 2011 the local 'settled' residents began complaining that the traveller 'problem' was worse than ever. With so many caravans parked on the road, without access to water or power, all sorts of sanitation and health problems manifested themselves. Trenches had been dug across Dale Farm to stop the travellers returning but the old cess pits leaked and there was a plague of rats. The digging of trenches also exposed industrial pollutants.

The costs to the public purse of the eviction are somewhat unclear. The estimate for the bailiffs alone was some £3million with additional funds furnished by central government. At the time of writing all the caravans on Oak Lane had gone. As for Dale Farm itself, it remains vacant.

Selected Bibliography

Abdel -Rahim, Moira, *Strike Breaking in Essex*, Canary Press, 2000.

Audley End a History, HMSO 1972.

Danger over Dagenham, Borough of Dagenham, 1947.

Barker, Juliet, *England Arise – The People, The King & The Great Revolt of 1381*. Little, Brown 2014.

Benham, H, *Essex at War*, Benhams of Colchester, 1945.

Begent, A. J, *Chelmsford at War*, Ian Henry, 1999.

Bowman, Martin. W, *US 9th Airforce Bases in Essex 1943-44*, Pen and Sword, 2010.

Clacton VCH Group, Clacton at War 1939-45, Clacton VCH Group 2003.

Cooper I, *Prisoner of War Camp 116 Hatfield Heath*, Hatfield Regis Local History Society, 2013.

Foley, M, *Essex Ready for Anything*, Sutton Publishing, 2006.

Free, Ken, *Camp 186 The Lost Town of Berechurch*, Amberly, 2010.

Fraser, Antonia, *The Warrior Queens, Boadicea's Chariot*, Phoenix Press, 1988.

Goodman, Anthony, *The Loyal Conspiracy*, Routledge & Kegan Paul, 1971.

Gordon, Dee, *Southend at War*, The History Press, 2010.

Groves, Reg, *Conrad Noel and the Thaxted Movement*, Redwood Press, 1967.

Hainsworth, R & Churches, C, *The Anglo –Dutch Naval Wars, 1652 – 1674*, Sutton Publishing Ltd, 1998.

Hill, Tony, *Guns and Gunners at Shoeburyness*, Baron Books, 1999.

Hilton, R.H, & Aston, *The English Rising of 1381*, Cambridge University Press, 1984.

Hunt, Richard, *Queen Boudica's Battle of Britain*, Spellmount, 2003.

Hussey, Frank, *Suffolk Invasion*, Terence Dalton Ltd, 1983.

Jackson, Robert, *de Havilland Mosquito*, Airlife Publishing, 2003.

Jones, J. R, *The Anglo-Dutch Wars of the Seventeenth Century*, Longman, 1996.

Kendrick, T. D, *The Vikings A History of*, Dover Publications Inc., 2004.

Lewin, Nicky, *Animal War, Brightlingsea 1995*, Firstsite,Colchester, 2000.

Liddell, W.H, & Wood, R.G, Wood, *Essex and the Great Revolt of 1381*, Essex Record Office, 1982.

Lockwood, M, *Essex Police, 'The End of the Phoney War*, Essex Police Museum.

Lindsay, Philip & Groves, Reg, *The Peasants' Revolt 1381*, Hutchinson, 1950.

Nash, Fred, *Survey of World War Two Defences in Southend-on-Sea Vol 2*, Southend Borough Council, 2001.

Noel, Conrad, *Conrad Noel, An Autobiography*, Dent and Sons, 1945.

Oram, Sir Charles, *The Great Revolt of 1381*, Greenhill Books, 1906.

Porter, K, & Wynn S, *German POW Camp 266, Langdon Hills*, Ukunpublished, 2012.

Quarmby, Katherine, *No Place to Call Home*, Oneworld, 2013.

Savage, Anne, *The Anglo Saxon Chronicles*, Tiger Books, 1995.

Times UK, *The Times Atlas of London*, Times Books, 2011.

Turner, R Frank & Steward Will, *The Maunsell Sea Forts, Part III*, F.R. Turner, 1996.

Valentine, Ian, *Station 43 Audley End and SOE's Polish Section*, Sutton, 2006.

ABOUT THE AUTHORS

ANDREW SUMMERS

Born within the sound of Bow Bells on a quiet day, Andrew has lived for the last 30 years in Hadleigh and been married to Glenis for 50 years. Andrew has bought books, sold books, printed books and now writes and publishes books too! Separately Andrew has edited *The Numbers Had to Tally* a Second World War survival story and written *They Did Their Duty, Essex Farm* which tells the story of Essex Farm in Belgium and its connections with the Essex Regiment. His latest work *The Last Flight of L33 and other stories from 1914 – 1918*, is available as an e-book.

JOHN DEBENHAM

Born in Romford, John has always lived in Essex. On retirement from engineering he took a BA History degree followed by an MA in Intellectual History, studying 'Civilisation and Barbarism'. He continues to enjoy historical research. A member of Southend Poetry Society, he writes poetry and short stories with longer works in 'perpetual progress'.

Also available from Essex Hundred Publications

Essex Hundred Publications

THE ESSEX HUNDRED HISTORIES
From the Roman sacking of Colchester to Ford's modern day wind turbines each chapter reflects the diversity of the county as well as showing the role Essex has played in the nation's development.
ISBN: 9780993108310 £8.99

THE ESSEX HUNDRED
The history of the county of Essex described in 100 poems and supported with historical notes and illustrations.
A unique book written by Essex poets covering 2,000 years of county history.
ISBN: 9780955229503 £7.99

MAGNA CARTA IN ESSEX
Essex barons were at the forefront of those who pushed hard for the Magna Carta, with Robert Fitzwalter, Lord of Dunmow appointed their leader. Yet within three months of the charter being sealed England was at war and Essex racked by conflict.
ISBN 9780993108303 £7.99

LONDON'S METROPOLITAN ESSEX
Events and Personalities, from Essex in London, which shaped the nation's history.
ISBN 9780955229558 £12.99

THE ESSEX HUNDRED CHILDREN'S COLOURING AND ACTIVITY BOOK
The Colouring and Activity Book is another title from the Essex Hundred family aimed at children and part written by children. The book includes not only Essex information but pictures to colour in, word searches, puzzles and questions.
ISBN: 9780955229534 £4.99

THEY DID THEIR DUTY, ESSEX FARM
Never Forgotten
Andrew Summers

A book that tells the story of Essex Farm, a First World War cemetery in Belgium, that will forever bear the county name, and its connections to the Essex Regiment.
ISBN 9780955229596 RRP £9.99

AEOLUS, Ruler of the Winds
by Shirley Baker

A whimsical story of sailing adventures around the Essex and Suffolk coast.
ISBN: 9780955229589 £7.99

THE NUMBERS HAD TO TALLY
by Kazimierz Szmauz

A World War II Extraordinary Tale of Survival
ISBN: 9780955229572 RRP £8.99

FULL CIRCLE
The Rise, Fall and
Rise of Horse Racing in Chelmsford
David Dunford
ISBN 9780993108358 £12.99

Digital Editions available

Essex Farm
The Numbers Had to Tally
L33 and other stories from WWI

Essex Hundred Publications.
Books written, designed and printed in Essex.
Available from bookshops, book wholesalers, direct from the publisher or online www.essex100.com